Pra

It is so easy to become ~~...........~~, ~~............~~ or is it the state of humanity? Maybe it's about how we choose to see things — the color of the glasses we wear. Maybe seeing the world differently, more positively, might be as simple as changing out the lenses. That is what this book can bring to your life; the path to changing out your lenses and showing you a world full of opportunity and wonder.

—GARY GARDIA, MED, LCSW, CT
End-of-Life Care Speaker/Consultant/Psychotherapist

With Perfect Circles, John Michael Stuart has given all of us permission to be perfectly imperfect. His story is one of tremendous challenge and great joy. It will leave you laughing and crying, and will help you realize that we all have perceived disabilities we can overcome. The book is, to borrow a new word I learned reading it, a wonderful "ZERP" that inspires, uplifts, and motivates!

—REVEREND DOUG FOGLESONG
Spiritual Life Center, Las Vegas, NV

John Michael Stuart's book is as inspiring as it is intelligent. I recommend it to anyone undergoing life's difficulties.

—STEVE MARTIN
Writer/Comedian/Actor

Perfect Circles is delightful, thought provoking, brutally honest, and funny all at the same time — very much like John! He helps people cope with unexpected limitations in their lives with an unparalleled empathy. In completing our circles, we touch our own humanity and thus recognize the humanity in others.

—MARY SPRIGGS
Registered Nurse

John's insight to the resiliency of the human spirit is amazing. Growing up as the lead singer of the Osmonds, I always pushed myself to perfection. Being labeled as the "One-take Osmonds," I spent most of my life with issues of self-acceptance even though I, unlike John, had been blessed with strong physical abilities. The message is the same no matter what gifts you possess or what your liabilities are. John encourages us to move past adversity and build upon your God-given talents. This book is one of the most insightful self-help books I've ever read. It's true when John states that the acceptance of ourselves has universal relevance to each one of us in finding true joy and contentment.

—MERRILL OSMOND
Entertainer

John Michael Stuart's book, Perfect Circles, is a deeply moving personal account of overcoming obstacles and making a life of value. It made me laugh; it made me cry; most of all, it made me think. It is the kind of book that is needed by anyone struggling to find his or her own path. You can't read it and be unmoved or unchanged. It is the best self-help book I have read in years—and I read them all!

—JUDI MOREO
Author, *You Are More Than Enough:
Every Woman's Guide to Purpose, Passion, & Power*

Perfect Circles

Redefining Perfection

Perfect Circles
Redefining Perfection

John Michael Stuart, MSW

Stephens Press • Las Vegas, Nevada

Editor: Jami Carpenter
Designer: Sue Campbell
Publishing Coordinator: Stacey Fott

13 12 11 10 09   1 2 3 4 5

Cataloging-in-Publication
Stuart, John Michael.
  Perfect circles : redefining perfection / John Michael Stuart.
  218 p. ; 23 cm.
ISBN: 1-935043-01-3
ISBN-13: 978-1-935043-01-0
  The author discusses the need for persons to accept themselves as they are, and work toward finding their own perfection regardless of physical disability, race, religion, or culture.
1. Self-Esteem. 2. People with disabilities. I. Title.
158.1 dc22   2009   2008937831

Post Office Box 1600
Las Vegas, NV 89125-1600

www.stephenspress.com

Printed in the United States of America

I dedicate this book to my loving mother and father who saw no limits to what I would accomplish along my life's journey.

Contents

Foreword — 13

Acknowledgements — 15

Introduction: *The Real Masterpiece* — 17

Chapter 1: *The Perfect Circle* — 23
Creating Our Own Perfect Circles
Maintaining Realistic Confidence
Being Open at the Top
Clearing the Junk
Discovering Our Perfect Circles Together
The Subjective Nature of Hope
Redefining "Perfect"
Conclusion

Chapter 2: *Those Majestic Moments* — 49
Moments of Bringing Truth Into Our Love
Awakening to Reality
Reality Check
The Decision to Act
Instilling Worth I Others
Get Up Off the Floor
Being Ourselves
Conclusion

Chapter 3: *How Far Down is Up?* — 67

Our Inner Navigational System

Addicted to Victimhood

Maintaining the Momentum

Passing on Perseverance

Conclusion

Chapter 4: *Holding the Vision* — 87

Holding the Collective Vision

Holding the Vision for Ourselves

Conclusion

Chapter 5: *The House of Cards* — 97

Growing From the Rubble

Hidden Treasures

Realizing Our Worth

The Power of Belief

The Forces of Time

Conclusion

Chapter 6: *Seeing the Lights* — 117

The Epidemic of Seeing Only the Negative

Keeping the Focus

Seeing the Good in Others

Expectations and Reality

Leaving Room for GrowthConclusion

Chapter 7: *The Light Habit* — 131

Having Appreciation for Life

Being Grateful for People in Our Lives

Being Grateful for What We Have

Conclusion

Chapter 8: *Becoming Perfectly Imperfect* — 143
Elevating Our Perspective
Accepting Differences
Breaking Free
Freeing Our "Perfect" Vision
Innovating Ourselves
Conclusion

Chapter 9: *Looking Beyond Ourselves* — 165
The Void That Tugs
Compassion is the Healer
Conclusion

Chapter 10: *Clearing the Way* — 181
Strengthening Relationships
Death: The Great Teacher
Initiating the Process
Conclusion

Chapter 11: *The Healing Power of Perspective* — 199
The Freedom to Choose
Conclusion

Chapter 12: *The Perfectly Imperfect Ending* — 211
The "Perfect" Paradox
Allowing "Perfect" to be Redefined
Completing the "Circle"
The Big Finish

About the Author — 217

Foreword

I FEEL IT a great privilege to have been asked by my nephew, John Michael Stuart, to write a foreword to his book, *Perfect Circles*.

I have known John from the day of his birth and have lived to rejoice in the what he has achieved and the person he has become. To read his book, *Perfect Circles*, is to be invited into the thoughtful, profound, humorous, self-introspective, touching, and open mind that is John's. His message is universal and timeless. What John teaches has been learned from own his life experiences and not from the writings of others.

John was born with cerebral palsy which affected his motor skills immediately. One of the great challenges of his life has been to live with the fact that because his motor skills have been affected, some people who don't really know him somehow believe he is also mentally-challenged. What a cross to bear for one as intelligent as John!

I must admit that I did not begin to develop a close relationship with John and appreciate what he had learned through his life until, at age fifty, I became paralyzed from the neck down and on life support as a result of a body surfing accident at Laguna Beach, California. Since that time, I have shared many special moments with John as we both have had to deal with what the world would think as not being the "best" of lifestyles.

John's book has deeply affected me. He has taken common events in his life, like trying to draw a perfectly round tire (the perfect circle), or hiking down the Grand Canyon, or describing the Las Vegas skyline, or watching the giant airliners take off and land, or trying to make a peanut butter and jelly sandwich, and has made of each experience a great and introspective lesson about life.

When I read of his experience of going to a regular high school, but in a bus for the handicapped, and being insulted and taunted because of his situation to the point that he would curl up on the floor of the bus to avoid the ridicule that surely would come his way each day, I began weeping and wondering where was I at that time in his life?

To me, John Michael Stuart is a world-class example of an individual who has not let his circumstances control his behavior. As you read the book, you sense how deeply he has thought about issues of self-worth, achievement, and what is really important in life. Not content to adopt a life of leisure, using his physical disability as an excuse for not achieving and blessing the lives of others, he graduated from college with a bachelor's degree and a master's degree in social work. I find it so wonderful, and somewhat ironic, that somebody in John's physical situation would choose a vocation involving "helping people with problems." His insights gained from working with hospice patients and their families are priceless.

John is a deep thinker; however, his deep thinking is so delightfully embedded in his real-life experiences that his profound message is extremely readable and enjoyable.

Taking the time to read *Perfect Circles* will enrich your mind and spirit, and help you see things in your own life from a different perspective, regardless of your physical capacities, religion, race, or culture.

—JACK L. RUSHTON, EdD
University of Southern California

Acknowledgements

I want to thank Ed Joyce and Trudy Marshall for the time and effort they put forth in editing this book and seeing the healing worth of its message.

The REAL Masterpiece

I was with some friends, walking through the New York Metropolitan Museum of Art, when I was given some amazing insights about life's experiences. We were casually making our way, admiring each masterpiece, when I overheard some comments that left me with some food for thought. While we were admiring the Picassos, surrounded by people who appreciated Picasso for how he could transform a blank canvas into a treasure of art, I heard someone wonder aloud how anyone in his right mind could consider this art — much less a masterpiece. I have to admit, this situation made me feel rather uneasy. Even though a genuine Picasso doesn't appeal to all people, it doesn't mean that it should be excluded from the honored category of being considered a genuine masterpiece. It's not so much what's painted on the canvas as much as it is the lens in which it is viewed. And so it is with how we view our life experiences.

Perspective matters! The lens in which we view ourselves is ultimately the same lens others will use to view us. After all, unless we can see our innate value, who else can? As with any great masterpiece, its creator has the obligation to first see the beauty in it before expecting others to do likewise.

When we are brought into this world, we are each figuratively accessorized with a blank canvas, a set of paints and a brush. Just as Picasso went about painting one-of-a-kind works of art, so is it our purpose to create one-of-a-kind lives.

Our most valued works of art are not hanging on a wall in a museum, but are manifested daily in the way we embrace the art of living. We are each the artist with the opportunity to masterfully shape our reality and absolutely no one is excluded from this dynamic process. Our unique creations are the lives we are living at this very moment. We need to know, with every fiber of our being, that we are works-in-progress, striving to evolve into something more. We engage in the masterful art of true living when we become conscious of the brush strokes we make against our canvases. If we are the artists, then we must be willing to transform our vision from seeing only random splashes of paint to seeing a creation of panoramic proportions. We must make the often difficult, and at times, painstaking effort to discover the well-hidden patterns made by each brush-stroke that come from our souls.

Picasso's paintings are worth millions to fine art connoisseurs — because they recognize that he was willing to share his art, even though others did not appreciate or even understand their intrinsic beauty. Not everyone walking through the museum of fine art is going to see beauty in every single painting and sculpture. Some, as I've mentioned, may even scoff when looking. But what matters most is that we, like Picasso, adopt the courage and vision to be the first to see the one-of-a-kind patterns that create purpose in our lives. We stunt this process when we don't allow our personal best to unfold as it was intended.

We can be the harshest critics of our own masterpieces to the point that we no longer have the ability to view them as such. If enough skilled artisans adopt this confining perspective, they will be unable to see the worth of their creations, as well as the creations of others. Unfortunately this has already happened in our society.

Many aspiring artists have taken a sabbatical, seeing their canvas as having little purpose. They leave it blank to avoid making any errors that would possibly label them as being less than perfect. Their paints and brushes are seen as insufficient to even start the creative process — much less complete their task. And so this epidemic starts to take its toll as we feel we not only lack the ability to become skilled artisans, but believe those with whom we share our world lack the skills as well. It is then that the human species hits an all-time low and our individual and collective sense of worth becomes extinct.

I have been in that place, feeling as if my own canvas had only imperfect blotches on it with no real pattern or purpose. Not only did I perceive my painting supplies left much to be desired, but I saw a big hole in my canvas that made it appear as if it was impossible to create anything that mattered. Creating a masterpiece was out of the question — or so it first appeared. Little did I realize at this low point of feeling like the victim that my life circumstances presented me with all the opportunities to put myself back in the ranks of the skilled artisans.

I was born breach. As a result, I was without oxygen for four minutes. In our day-to-day lives, four minutes doesn't seem to be a significant amount of time; but in my case, this insignificant time lapse had an impact not only on me — but also for all those who would love and include me in their lives.

For the rest of my life, I would live with the physical disability known as cerebral palsy, a neurological disorder that affects the part of the brain that controls the physical body functions. I not only look different, but I have difficulty using my hands in performing tasks like eating and writing. My feet turn inward when I walk and sometimes I fall. My speech is slurred and labored. These challenges would have a profound impact on not only how I was able to perform physical tasks, but on how I would relate to the world around me. It would ultimately impact all aspects of my life. But more importantly, it would bring me insights that are uniquely my own, as I have learned how to allow life's adversities make me stronger.

The big insight and treasure I have received in living in a physically disabled body is that it can be limiting and even a tragedy if I perceive it from that vantage point. The hole in my canvas was present because I chose to perceive its existence.

A truth that has become crystal clear to me through the years of living with adversity is that it's not what happens to us that impairs our ability to truly live; it's what we are willing to learn about ourselves and each other that will ultimately strengthen us along the way. Such a gem has been of insurmountable value. I wouldn't trade my life with that of anyone else.

The perceived holes in our lives can be the very learning experiences, that if seen differently, allow for considerable personal growth and the realization of our potential. Treasures of any immense worth are often difficult to find, but once they finally are, we will have to admit it was well worth our effort.

The stories in this book are not meant to stir heartache or sympathy, but rather to connect us to that innermost part of our being — the human spirit that we all innately possess. It is the human spirit, our inner Picasso, which can only see a canvas with a picture painted upon it with beauty, purpose, and unending potential.

We all are represented by the individual fine works of art that are deserving of our admiration, not for being exactly the same as the next, but for so eloquently demonstrating our uniqueness. The only difference is that we're not yet a finished work hanging on a wall, collecting dust in a museum, but a dynamic, living work-in-progress.

We must *never* neglect to look through the lens of the skilled artisan, knowing that we already have all the tools we need to continue working to create more than a blank canvas — a canvas with a true masterpiece drawn upon it. It is through this lens that I write this book. May we all discover our GEMS of great worth!

To be what we are, and to become what we are capable of becoming, is the only end to life.

—SPINOZA

Chapter 1

The Perfect Circle

IN WANTING TO select an appropriate theme for this book, I recalled one of my past experiences when I was about nine or ten. This experience may seem rather ordinary, but it is significant because it gave me valuable insight into the importance of self-acceptance. Through the years, I have realized that building genuine self-acceptance begins in childhood.

My schoolmates and I liked to see who could draw the wildest imaginable revved-up racing cars. Our pictures displayed cars with big tires, exaggerated chrome exhaust pipes and bright red flames painted on the side. We could not wait to show each other what we had drawn the day before. The school day seemed to be preoccupied with this macho boyhood artistic expression. Since our teacher would restrict this activity to play time, we would eagerly start creating our automotive expressions at home after homework. If it were left up to us, we would have gone straight for the brightly colored crayons — if our parents permitted; but that was seldom the case.

I remember sitting down at my desk with the full intention of creating a masterpiece from start to finish. First, I would draw the chassis with all the fancy racing accessories: flames, bright colors, and exhaust included. To finish my masterpiece, I would draw big tires in the rear and little ones in the front to exaggerate that this car was only meant for winning the race. Because my hands were unsteady, due to the cerebral palsy, my lines were never perfectly straight nor my circles perfectly round. Though the lines that were drawn to create the car's chassis were always imperfectly straight, somehow I could always look beyond these imperfections to see the artistic value that lay underneath. But when it came to drawing the tire circles, I couldn't tolerate it unless they were perfectly round. So as I was about to finish my masterpiece, I would draw two non-perfectly round circles, representing tires, and my pride would quickly turn to anger, then disgust, as the imperfect tires had absolutely ruined what I had been anticipating to be the perfect race car drawing. I would then shred the picture into what seemed to be a million little pieces, sending myself, and all others, a clear message that I only accepted absolute perfection. When meeting my friends to share our pictures, I would almost always come empty-handed as my artwork that I so eagerly wanted to show them was lying in the trash. The high level of expectation I had imposed on myself made it almost impossible to create anything from start to finish. Even more importantly, it prevented me from finding joy and satisfaction in what I was creating.

I was teaching myself the destructive habit of self-ridicule and non-acceptance. Soon those habits became ingrained in me. This childhood behavior became the basis and theme for much of my life — until I was willing to go through the effort to change. Even now, in my adult years, self-acceptance has been a hurdle that has been far more difficult to overcome than any physical limitations.

Looking back, I now realize that if I had accepted my imperfect tire circles, I would have, in all probability, avoided many of the difficult lessons in the vital importance of self-acceptance. I have painfully discovered, through the school of hard-knocks, aka "life," true joy is achieved by enjoying the journey instead of being preoccupied with the minor details along the way. Before we can overcome any of our challenges and hurdles, we must first learn to accept the abilities and strengths we already possess. Yes, surprisingly enough, we all have difficulty in discovering and accepting our innate abilities. We ruminate so much on our limitations, both perceived and real, that we ignore our strengths and unique gifts. Our special talents and gifts are never revealed and shared as they were intended. This behavior will continue until we finally look in the right place, within ourselves!

We all draw incomplete race cars when we refuse to accept those things that don't look exactly as we had originally envisioned them. We almost finish our "car chassis" or masterpiece, by putting on the finishing touches, only to throw the whole thing away because the tires aren't round enough. Our race cars don't even have a chance to roll off the assembly line to win the race. We all draw imperfect circles in life. We all have flaws of one kind or another. As soon as we accept this sometimes unpleasant reality, we can get back on the race track. Only then can our imperfect circles be transformed into "perfect" ones.

Creating Our Own Perfect Circles

PERFECT CIRCLES, THE title and basis for this book, symbolizes self-acceptance. Our circles do not have to be perfectly round and geometrically measured with a compass guiding our hand for exact precision, just as our lives do not have to be perfectly ordered and precise. But this does not mean that we face life's situations carelessly, with no desire to expand and improve ourselves, taking on a defeatist attitude. In fact, it's quite the opposite. We must be willing to face challenges in life, making every sincere attempt to leap those hurdles that confront us, creatively adapting to our unique abilities.

When we creatively adapt, we discover what strengths and attributes we already possess, and learn how we can use them for our long term growth and benefit. We don't have to be someone we're not, because who we are at this very moment is enough to become all that we are meant to be. We have all the tools we need at the present moment. All we have to do is, first, discover that they do in fact exist; and then second, be willing to use them. The tools will indeed vary from one individual to the next to enable us to make our own "Perfect Circle" or one of-a-kind contribution to the world. And just as we create our literal circles with their different sizes and shapes, no two being alike, so we create our own unique lives. Although we may do things different than the person next to us, we do them well by being our personal best. We are as different as the circles we draw, each as perfect as the next.

To begin the process of creating "Perfect Circles," we must first be realistic about our abilities and even our disabilities. We must realize that they are what makes up our unique wholeness. There is absolutely nothing wrong or pessimistic with being realistic, because we can make reality fit into our dreams and aspirations. We may even find that our reality is not as bad as it seems. It may even be our number one asset in helping us shape ourselves into who we want to be. Just because we don't all have the ability to be brain surgeons doesn't mean we lack talents for something else of equal importance and value to the world. If we discover it would be best to *keep our hands off the scalpel*, we should use this as an opportunity to investigate deeper into those areas we can excel while feeling a sense of purpose. To say that we don't have a contribution to make means we're not looking hard enough to find it. We should not stand for such excuses! More often than not, putting preconceived expectations on how our individual circles should look limits their potential to become what they are meant to be. And like the race car, our dreams and aspirations are thrown away before they're completed — because of our impatience, judgments, and misconceptions we not only place on ourselves but each other.

Keep Your Hands Off the Scalpel

WHILE DECIDING ON a professional career, I felt that I would find the greatest emotional fulfillment in a profession that would allow me to assist others in overcoming their own challenges and adversities. Perhaps this was my way of giving back to all those people who had helped and encouraged me throughout my own life.

The first thing that came to my mind was to apply to medical school and become a doctor. I shared my desire with family and friends. In explaining to me that they had the greatest trust in me, they made it very clear that they would hardly consider me to perform a brain or heart procedure on them or anyone who remotely possessed life. They recommended strongly that I keep my hands off the scalpel or anything else remotely sharp for that matter.

Nursing was out of the question. I can hardly hold still long enough for someone to get an adequate blood pressure reading on me, let alone take someone else's. And giving shots was also off limits.

After reviewing further options, I discovered that the field of social work met all my needs, emotionally as well as physically. I knew without a shadow of a doubt that my particular physical circumstances would create no limitations in my newly-selected profession. The pay, although not as robust as a doctor's, met my financial needs and I would still be fulfilling my number one requirement, helping others. In some instances, I'd be working right alongside doctors and nurses as a valuable team member. And best of all, those closest to me gave me a vote of confidence; they would come to me without a bit of hesitation if they ever needed a social worker — without feeling their lives were in danger.

Creatively defining ourselves demands that we get rid of any preconceived ideas that restrict us and limit our ability to think outside the box so that we can begin focusing on what we can do instead of what we can't. With this shift in perspective, I pursued an alternative route; and in 1997, I received my master's degree in social work from the University of Nevada, Las Vegas. Since then, I have successfully worked as a case manager in both hospital and hospice settings, doing what brings me joy, helping others.

Maintaining Realistic Confidence

OFTEN, BEING REALISTIC provides the greatest channel for achieving our desires — as long as we keep those desires and goals in focus. The great thing about looking at facts is that we will find our genuine strengths in those areas we can truly excel in, rather than setting ourselves up for disappointment and defeat. But the road to creatively adapting can be rough as we are faced with ideas and opinions of those who lack the confidence in us. Some of our most difficult hurdles are put before us when those who appear to be the experts tell us that our goals are not real or attainable. Giving too much credibility to any one source can restrict the vision we hold for ourselves. We must be persistent in getting acquainted with our own abilities so that the confidence we build can stand strong when realistic measurements are used to challenge our dreams and belief systems. Even the people who we admire in their areas of expertise can sometimes be wrong. Why? Because they're human!

When these people use their map of reality, often it is just that, *their* map, which is not always accurate. Sometimes they're totally off-base; "their map" becomes, at best, their "perception." We have a responsibility to ourselves and each other to conduct a reality check to see what is real and what is not, what is attainable and what is not. Reality can be on our terms if we have the courage to welcome it to our side and not fear it or push it away.

In 1530, the Polish astronomer Nicolaus Copernicus discovered the sun was at the center of the galaxy and the earth revolved around it, not the other way around — as it was firmly believed at the time. Copernicus had such courage and vision that he went against the grain of the teachings of the religious institution that had a monopoly on the truth in that time. Even though Copernicus was labeled a heretic, he wouldn't back down on revising what is now "our map," placing the sun at the center of the Milky Way and holding all the other planets in its orbit. We can thank our lucky stars for his courage to see reality as it truly is or we would still believe everything revolves around us. The ability to look beyond mere perceptions, looking at observable facts, is the first step in the initiation to overcome.

Initiation to Overcome

DURING THE COURSE of earning a master's degree, one of my professors invited me to speak privately with her in her office. She proceeded to tell me in a rather solemn, heartfelt way how I would never be able to make it in the social work profession because no one would ever give credibility to someone with a disability. She apologized for having to break the news of what she thought was the reality I would face as a physically disabled person. She tried to apologize on my behalf for the time and energy I had already spent in school. At that point in time, I had already been in college for about two and-a-half years.

She continued to console me, as she stated, "After all, we social workers have to be realistic with each other. That's our ethical professional responsibility." This statement made me feel as though I was being initiated and kicked out of "the club" at the same time. She then informed me there would be no social service agency that would even be willing to hire me. Being that she was not only my professor with the letters "PHD" after her name, but also the chairperson of the entire social work department, I started to give an incredible amount of weight to her perception about my professional future and abilities.

There I was, in one of the most important examinations of my academic career, and in all probability, my life. There were no classrooms or textbooks involved, but rather, an informal meeting between two individuals: one, the well-credentialed professor; the other, her eager young student trying to earn his own way and succeed in a new career. And now he just found out that the profession and future clients would never be able to accept him because of a physical disability. At that very moment, whether or not the teacher knew it, I realized I was a student in the classroom of life who was being examined on the integrity of my self-confidence — not just my obvious physical impairments.

I was required to respond positively to one imperative question from within the deepest part of my being: Had I built up enough self-confidence to honestly believe I was fully capable of accomplishing what I had already set out to do? My response would not only determine the outcome of the vision I held for myself, but would also bring to the forefront how much I could depend on myself for personal navigation.

This was not something that I could pull the correct answer from a textbook or even from someone who I thought was more intelligent and had all the correct answers for my life. I was required to answer it for myself — from the prior knowledge I had accumulated through each life experience. Only this would give me a clearer picture of what I was truly capable of becoming.

By this time, I had already demonstrated to myself my ability to successfully interact with patients and their families — while being a student and interning at a local rehabilitation hospital. I had already received a near perfect score on a quarterly internship evaluation from the hospital supervisor who had observed my professional abilities. Instead of validating the outdated beliefs about myself by hastily concluding that the person with the distinguished letters "PhD" after her name was right, while I was living in some sort of fantasyland, I was now able to move forward as I had originally intended without questioning myself — as I had so frequently done in the past.

I felt as if I had just passed one of life's most important tests — with flying colors! I had just broken a behavioral pattern that was stunting my growth: giving into the viewpoints of others. As with all of life, these important life-exams, that we all eventually take, administered in the least likely of places, require our strictest attention. Ultimately, only each of us, individually, can truly know what we're capable of.

Looking back at particular times in my life, I can vividly recall instances when others would tell me I couldn't do something and then I successfully did it anyway. There were those who told me I couldn't even go to college, much less get my master's and then, there I was, actually doing it! I also recall not going after my ambitions because someone else told me I couldn't; only later to regret having listened. Sometimes a little bit of personal stubbornness goes a long way. By not allowing others to place their preconceived limitations on me, not only did I become a social worker, I would be, disability and all, a great one.

Being Open at the Top

To absorb other's counsel, we have to take a balanced approach, at the same time knowing when it is not applicable to our life. I have made it a practice to be teachable when others give me their input, especially when they may have more knowledge or expertise in a particular area. In fact, if we are resistant to new information, we shut down our ability to learn and expand upon who we are in the process of becoming. I have to admit that my own stubbornness in failing to give heed to wise counsel has thrown me some curveballs. It is indeed healthy to adopt humility into our lives, leaving ample room for the power to transfer from one person to the next. After all, one of the greatest philosophers of all time, Socrates, once said, "I know that I know nothing."

To be truly teachable, we must be open at the top, to take in new information while filtering through that which we already know about ourselves. This means that we learn all that we can through wise and even the unwise counsel of others and then filter that information through our own experiences and observations. To effectively do this, we must be in the ongoing state of mind to form a solid foundation of confidence — with enough strength that it doesn't falter or crumble under external pressure. It is only then that we can process new information to see if it corresponds to what we already affirmatively know and believe about ourselves and are in the process of becoming. An honest and up front self-inventory is not only necessary, but imperative, if we are truly going to discover what our strengths and capabilities are and that we can say with confidence we truly possess.

Clearing the Junk

Our personal filters are screens, imbedded in our minds, that comprise the beliefs we hold about ourselves and the world around us. Any new incoming information is interpreted through this screen — what we already think we know, both about ourselves and our world. I can personally testify that when my filter is cluttered with junk, negative self-talk, and beliefs that lead to cynicism, it is ineffective and, in most cases, detrimental to my continued physical and emotional growth and well-being. The negative clutter and junk that accumulated throughout my years from negative self-talk turned inward, like man-made chemical waste washing up on the seashore, always manifested itself in my outward negative actions. I would only believe people if they told me what I couldn't do or become; because, after all, I was feeding myself these same messages.

If there were those who told me I could become anything I wanted, I would immediately discard their encouragement as nonsense, since it didn't correspond to the negative beliefs I was refusing to reevaluate and let go. In wanting to deal in actual facts, the only fact I was failing to deal with was that my confining thoughts and beliefs about my own capabilities posed far greater limitations than any physical disability ever could. In order to begin to move forward at all, I had to clear away the junk that was in the way. The ageless wisdom, *as a man thinketh, so is he,* validates the fact that life experiences are not always a result of what happens to us, but are created by the way we think.

As We Thinketh

THOSE WHO HAVE known me for a while have made personal observations concerning my improved mobility, hand and arm coordination, as well as my speech, over the years. In retrospect, and through my own observations, I believe their assessment is correct. I was unable to write legibly using either a pen or pencil. I was trained to use a typewriter at a very young age. I vividly remember sitting at the typewriter trying to not only learn where each key was located on the keyboard, but struggling just to hit each key. My hands would slip off the keyboard so often I had to start using an apparatus that fit on my head, like a cap, with a long metal arm/pointer that extended down to the keys. Then I could hit each key by using my head. When eating, I would also need help. My arms would shake uncontrollably. My knees and joints gave me so much pain that sometimes I needed to use a wheelchair. Those around me could see the negative effects of cerebral palsy that manifested themselves in my daily life.

Then after about my third year of undergraduate school, my abilities steadily improved. I began to start using my hands to feed myself, use the typewriter, and later, the computer, without the use of any kind of apparatus. The need for a wheelchair became less frequent as my aches and pains subsided and my speech became clearer! My words became more pronounced. Given my medical knowledge of my neurological condition, it neither gets progressively worse or better from the time of onset. What could be attributed to this steady improvement through the years? Why did this happen?

I believe this physical improvement came from a simple shift in my perspective. I now know that our thinking does have a profound effect on the physical functioning of our bodies. I personally observed that as my thoughts and attitude changed, so did my body. My inward state outwardly manifested itself. If my inner emotional world was trembling or falling apart, my outward one would follow its helpless lead. If I told myself that I was nothing more than a helpless victim of circumstance with the inability to achieve what I wanted out of life, that became my reality. Conversely, if I told myself that I was capable of achieving what I wanted, not allowing a disability to get in the way, then that became my reality. As with us all, mind does lead body.

This is the ultimate meaning behind discovering our "Perfect Circle" — accepting what is already perfect within us, creatively adapting ourselves around that innate perfection, while also allowing ourselves to accept our differences and imperfections. Self-accepting our differences are the healing balm for the body and spirit as we allow them to purify our personal filters so that encouraging, uplifting thoughts can not only be heard loud and clear, but cemented into the very core of our being. It's no wonder that medical science is finally taking notice *as a man thinketh, so is he.*

Discovering Our "Perfect Circles" Together

"Perfect Circles" represent our wholeness as we each discover our unique contributions to the world without the need to compare ourselves with others. They are the circles we draw with our own abilities, without judgment or self-condemnation. They are our unique symbols of self-worth, like our fingerprints; our imprints on the world. Only by the acceptance of our own "Perfect Circles" do we have the capacity to positively influence and accept others as they are. Whether we know it or not, when we strive to discover our own unique wholeness, we help others to discover their unique wholeness, thereby transforming the world into a better place to be.

Collectively we can assist in the self-discovery of wholeness in one another through the powerful influence of living our unique stories of overcoming adversity. Individually, we are the author responsible for writing our own life stories and destinies. Together we can facilitate recognition of the resiliency within us all that is enduring and ever expanding. Discovering our "Perfect Circles" can be a collective exercise, influencing each of us trying to discover our own.

The quote, "When the student is ready, the teacher will appear" is a daily phenomenon, as we are interchangeably the teacher and student throughout our life's journey. The stories we tell are the lessons that are taught and learned about the life-affirming power of the human spirit.

This process plays such an important part in our life's purpose. Building each other up, instead of tearing down, as we aspire to discover our "Perfect Circles" is like our personal magic wand that is capable of transmitting the Magic "Zerp," the power we all possess to encourage one another.

Mrs. Kitchen's Magic "ZERP"

I WAS ONCE invited by a seventh grade school teacher, Mrs. Kitchen, to speak to her classes about the challenges associated with living with and overcoming a physical disability. Little did I realize that Mrs. Kitchen and her students would teach me about the amazing power we each possess to influence other lives for the better. I realized that the subject matter she was teaching was not part of the standard, reading, writing, and arithmetic curriculum, but one that most fail to credit as having any importance in our educational system. The classes I would have the privilege of speaking to were part of a pilot program designed to help underprivileged kids in inner-city schools raise their self-esteem.

What an incredible program this was! It included the teaching of such life-skills as goal setting, visioning, and the basic coping strategies needed to succeed in life. In the short time I had become acquainted with Mrs. Kitchen, I learned there could have not been a person better qualified to attempt to influence and change lives. After spending time with her students, I only slightly grasped the magnitude of the challenges she faced in trying to make a positive difference in students who had either been or were in an inner-city gang or felt powerless over their lives. If they weren't directly involved in a gang, they either had a friend or sibling who was. In many cases, their acquaintances and relatives had died. They talked about it as if it were the norm.

In just the few hours I spent with these kids, they opened up to me, telling me of their broken lives and feelings of hopelessness for their futures. Even the known class bully broke down his rough and tough exterior walls to tell me his despair of living in a broken home and recently attending the funeral of his older brother, who died from a bullet wound from a rival gang. He assured me his fate would surely be no different.

This class was not special because it taught a curriculum on the cutting edge for inner-city middle schools, but rather, it was extraordinary because of a teacher who brought her vision for positive change to each of her students. Before speaking to each new group of students, Mrs. Kitchen briefed me on the individual personalities that made each group unique. For her, the students she taught were not grim reminders of an increase in a hopeless new generation; instead, they were examples of human beings who wanted to meet their maximum potential and make valuable contributions, but needed encouragement and a vision of a future filled with opportunities, and above all, someone who was willing to give them hope. She projected desperately-needed hope to every class, along with a firm belief that no matter how dire their circumstances may have appeared, change was always a distinct possibility. At the beginning of each period, Mrs. Kitchen would bring out her beautifully decorated magic wand, accessorized with sparkling streamers and glitter to give out what she and everyone knew to be a "ZERP."

It was explained to me that a "ZERP" was just a nonsensical term that signified a tap-on-the-head by the glittering wand. It had proven time and time again to ease one's troubles and pain. At first, I thought to myself that the whole exercise would seem rather juvenile to a group of seventh graders, especially to ones who had seen and actually been involved in the cold and cruel world of violence. I was way off-the-mark! As her students rolled in, half of them would immediately form a line to receive their "ZERP." Yes, I actually saw the rough and tough class bully eagerly waiting to get a tap from the pretend magic wand. I saw faces go from showing sadness and despair to brightness and joy with just one tap of something made of ordinary sparkles and plastic. It seemed like magic!

What I was privileged and highly honored to witness that day was not magic at all, but a real miracle that each of us is capable of performing. The glittering wand did not hold the power. It was a committed school teacher determined to be an influence for good in the lives of those who were in desperate need.

I did get an opportunity to tell how I managed to live with and overcome the obstacles associated with my particular disability. I pray that I was in some small way an agent for change in someone's life that day. But far more significant than my small role was witnessing how just one person, who had every reason to be cynical and discouraged, who might think that she could not make a difference, never gave up on hope, or in this case, never put away the magic wand that changed her kids lives — if only for the moment, day, or better yet, lifetime. Hope and vision is contagious! If only we are willing to spread it around as did Mrs. Kitchen.

Some time later, I heard from this amazing teacher that funding for her class had been eliminated. She called to tell me that the school board felt it could not be definitively determined through qualitative measurements whether or not her class that taught the importance of self-worth had any impact on bringing about positive change. I wanted so much to go before that board and tell them how just one "ZERP" could transform a face showing despair and even fear into one that was brighter and more hopeful. Unfortunately, the hope and positive influences we are capable of each projecting into the visible world are like atoms and molecules that cannot be observed with the naked eye, the basic building blocks that make up all we can see in the physical world.

Our influence and what we project to those around us in the form of hope and encouragement are two of the most basic building blocks of the human spirit. The term "ZERP," as ridiculous as it may sound to us or even a group of seventh graders, had the power to transform lives. I was quite angered that a group of board members would abolish funding for what I believe to be a vital piece of curriculum that builds the invisible but very necessary foundation of the human spirit. After all, are we going to get rid of atoms and molecules just because we can't see them? Such an impossible feat would dissolve the entire universe. I now realize that it wasn't this particular class or pilot program that produced the magic behind the "ZERP," but rather, it was one person's vision and expectation of what others could become that made the difference.

When I last talked to Mrs. Kitchen some years ago, she promised me that no matter what the method, she would never stop giving out her magical "ZERP." What a lesson we can learn from her! Cutting-edge programs don't make the difference. People do!

The Subjective Nature of Hope

The hope and quality of life we each possess cannot be held up to an objective standard, as it is purely subjective in nature. Throughout my life, there have been people who have told me that they had a physical disability or knew someone who did and knew exactly what it was like to be in my body. The truth is that no matter how well-intentioned these people are, they do not know what it's like to be in my body — nor do I know what it's like to be in theirs. We may share some commonalities and even the same types of disabilities and limitations, but ultimately, only we ourselves know how we process these similarities and that of which we are individually capable. We each have our own idea of what hope and an acceptable quality of life looks like and no one can define it for us. There is no agreed-upon single set of discreet measurements.

Sometimes the people in our lives want to relate to our particular set of circumstances and challenges, when, in reality, they can only relate using their own set of emotions and coping mechanisms. One person told me that if he had to contend with my particular set of physical challenges he would want to end his life by putting a bullet through his head. At first I didn't know if this comment was meant to compliment my resiliency or as a hint that I should be put out of my misery.

After contemplating it for a while, I realized it was neither. It was this particular person's personal view of my reality through his personal experience lens. He could do nothing more than guess how he would respond if he were in my shoes. But he wasn't in my shoes and couldn't possibly see what I saw or feel what I feel. In my reality, having a physical disability has in no way diminished my quality of life, much less diminished it to the point of wanting to end it. While this individual may have felt he would take such drastic actions if he were me, I seriously doubt that he would have. No one really knows his own level of resiliency until he is put to the challenge. Owning feelings of hope or hopelessness are choices to be made and we are free to choose either one. Ultimately, only we can know what our "Perfect Circle" looks like and absolutely no one can draw or experience it for us.

In working with patients so ill that they are confined to bed, I have observed how one's definition of an acceptable quality of life cannot be defined by a concrete set of criteria that we all agree upon. Family members will often comment how their ill loved ones would be better off dead as they are no longer able to find meaning or enjoyment in life given their current state of health. What these families don't realize is that the measurements used to determine both hope and quality of life change with one's circumstance. Patients whose lives appear to be over have indicated their biggest joy still comes from seeing their grandchildren grow up or someday feeling well enough to eat their favorite food again. At one point in their lives, these simpler things may have seemed routine, but now are the very experiences that bring enough joy into their world that makes it worth living — even under new unfortunate sets of circumstances. Many people who are ill and close to death find joy and gratitude in the smallest, simplest things in life. Their measurement of hope and quality of life broadens to include more of what defines it. I've heard people who have survived life-threatening illnesses say that everyone should temporarily be in such a state of health, because such a state brings with it an opportunity to get a heightened sense of joy and appreciation from the simpler things that were always there but were never noticed. We finally discover what's really important in life.

Since that which defines hope and quality of life varies from one person to the next, it is up to us to look deeper into our individual set of circumstances to discover our own subjective measurements. In doing this, we can stand firm when people offer their opinions and advice, knowing with surety what our picture of hope, purpose, and meaning to life looks and feels like. In looking back over my life, I can vividly recall times when I let the negative opinions of others draw me into a state of discouragement and even despair because I did not have my own set of measurements that would help me define my hope. I could not stand firm and confident on what I believed about my own strengths and I was allowing others to define them for me.

Modern advances in technology and in medical science have made our subjective measurements of quality of life vitally important. Today, we have the option of having our life extended by means of "heroics" or artificial life support. I have had patients on renal dialysis in order to maintain their kidney function say they still enjoyed life. In fact, while working as a social worker in a dialysis center, I saw people lead very productive and fulfilling lives, even though they were required to come to the center three and sometimes four days a week. Many went on to receive successful kidney transplants and could stop treatment. Some of my family and friends, after knowing I worked at a dialysis center, would say they didn't know what they would do if they were in such a situation. And you know what? They don't know what they would do, and neither do I, until we are there ourselves. But for the many I had the privilege of knowing, dialysis didn't interfere with their "Perfect Circle."

Technological advances give rise to more of life's choices. One of these choices is to determine for ourselves when or when not to be use "heroics" — defining for ourselves when the quality of life begins and ends. Yes, as we have the access to the technology to extend our lives, we also have the right to decide when and when it is not appropriate to use it. There are those who see life-support as "not viable" when conscious awareness is lost, or if life can no longer be measured as "worth living." For these people, having a peaceful ending to this life completes their "Perfect Circle."

The decisions we make concerning what we will do at the end of life not only affects us but all those with whom we are associated. We are each affected in a variety of ways, tugging at the very core of our being as we are forced to let go. No matter what our fears, insecurities, or judgments are, we must be able to stand with courage and allow others to define their own subjective measurements of what hope and a quality-of-life looks like for them, not us. Our role is to extend support to those making these difficult decisions, keeping in the forefront of our minds the worth of each individual as we submit to hope.

Submitting to Hope

As a social worker, working in hospice and hospital settings, I've often discussed quality of life issues with patients and their families. It was my professional obligation to make sure that those under my care were fully aware of their right to have an Advanced Directive. This is a legally binding document enabling individuals to proclaim for themselves, in advance, whether or not they desire "heroics" or life support to be used to keep them alive. It also allows a representative, a loved one, or close friend to be appointed in advance who knows one's subjective measurements in order to determine what quality-of-life is remaining for them.

By having such a directive, important medical decisions can be made on behalf of the patients while honoring their consciously made choices. Such a document becomes legally enforced if one's quality-of-life should be compromised and the injured or ill party is unable to make his desires immediately known to those in charge of his care. Each of us has the right if we are of sound mind and of the required age to have an Advanced Directive to declare our own end-of-life desires.

While we may not have the ability to prevent a tragic accident or chronic illness, we do have the ability to choose how we will live if heroics are required to sustain our life. All health care providers have the legal obligation to inform us of these important rights.

This entire process necessitates one's own subjective measurement of quality versus quantity-of-life to be thought out as each determines for himself when is an acceptable time to die. In more times than not, I found that most people are reluctant to even think about what they would or would not do in an end-of-life situation — much less put it in writing. But there are those who do exercise their right and take a serious look at what they want done if there is a time their definition of quality of life has been compromised. They are the ones who aren't willing to leave these matters in the hands of those who don't know their wishes.

While working as a social worker in a rehabilitation hospital, I was asked to make sure all patients either knew about or had an Advanced Directive in their medical records. It was then that I came across a patient record of a 71-year-old man who was comatose and being kept alive by a gastrointestinal feeding tube. The odd thing was that he had an Advanced Directive that he had drawn up two years prior, in the front of his medical record, clearly showing his desire not to be put on any kind of life support. I was told that this man's family was contesting his decision not to be on life support. After further investigation, I found that he had been estranged from his younger sister who had not talked to him in over seven years due to ill feelings regarding his choice of lifestyle. In her mind's eye, this had somehow impaired his ability to make his own decisions. When he was competent, this man, who could no longer speak for himself, had already appointed a legal representative, someone he dearly loved and respected to be at his side, ready to speak on his behalf.

The appointed representative was more than able to fulfill his responsibility. I brought my concerns to the hospital's director of social services — that this patient's wish and right not to be on life support may have been compromised. She made it very clear that the agency's position was to side with the family and leave the feeding tube in place — fearing legal repercussions if they did not. It was also made clear that my employment would be in jeopardy if I pushed the issue any further. It was then I investigated issues of patients' rights and my obligation to safeguard them. Of course, I didn't want to jeopardize my employment or the company that gave it to me. There I was, facing the first ethical dilemma of my fairly new career, one that was only talked about in the academic vacuum of textbooks and classrooms, but one I had never before experienced. As I went back to reference the academic journals of ethical social work practice, the one overriding principle that stood out was the need to uphold one's right to self-determination. The journal spelled out, very clearly, that in situations like these, a person's right to self-determination was to be protected and upheld irrespective of corporate insecurities and outside judgment calls. In this case, I was supposed to advocate for the client's subjective measurements of an acceptable quality of life the he had previously determined for himself when he was legally able to so do.

This was no longer school or practice. This was real life and death with another's life hanging in the balance. I had to decide on what platform I was going to stand. To protect the rights of a human being or, a company that appeared to be violating those rights.

I had to remember why I first chose my new profession. To help and stand up for others as they had helped and stood up for me when I was unable to myself. I vividly recalled how my eleventh grade English Literature teacher went to bat for me. She advocated for me to be in her class when the guidance counselors wanted me to be in the remedial classes they thought were more conducive to my learning capacity. But I wasn't mentally challenged; I wanted to be in her class. I wanted to learn about the great writers of all times. I knew I would succeed. They hadn't taken the time or energy to truly get to know me and my abilities as another unique human being striving to reach his maximum potential. They were, in a sense, asleep at the wheel, on auto pilot taking them through the motions of what they were supposed to be doing — standing up for those who couldn't yet do it for themselves. I am truly grateful for that eleventh grade teacher having the courage for not going to sleep on me.

Yes, it takes courage to stand up for another, sometimes mandating us to go against the grain. It may seem so much easier to just exist, meeting minimal expectations and at the end of the day or at the conclusion of our lives, go home, having made no difference in someone else's life. Just think, if Hitler's men would have had the courage to stand up for what was right, millions of lives would have been spared and a horrible demonstration of human cruelty would not be in our history books.

And so, as this lifeless person lay before me, with only artificial nutrition keeping him alive, knowing he had already proclaimed for himself never to be in such a position, my decision on what platform I would stand on became quite obvious.

To no avail, I tried to reason with my superiors. They reminded me who I was supposed to be going to bat for and it wasn't for the people in our care. It was then I thought I could stand on both platforms, satisfying everyone, except maybe for the estranged family members. I went through the appropriate channels to keep everyone involved, yet out of harm's way, by calling in a consultant from the county Senior Advocacy Office. Perhaps the consultant could resolve this human rights issue while keeping my employer out of litigation. Hopefully, a government agency would surely do the right thing. It did.

After the advocate's office discovered this man's legally binding desires, his gastrointestinal feedings were immediately ordered to be discontinued. Three days later, he died.

I thought my employer would applaud my decision, since the county took complete responsibility for this man's death and relieved my employer of its responsibility of doing the right thing — doing what he wanted. To my surprise, the director called me in and told me I was not a team player and he would have to terminate my employment!

He didn't specifically bring up the afore-noted incident as the justification to fire me. Rather, he said the office had received "several complaints," and it would be dangerous for the company to retain me. Since no prior complaints had been brought to my attention, I could only guess that I was not a team player by practicing ethical social work and upholding my patient's right to self-determination — all within the bounds of the law as I was taught in the textbooks.

As I left the job, I felt a sense of purpose, because I had done the right thing! I had transcended my insecurities of potentially losing my job, which I ultimately did, to feel and know why I chose the profession I did. I discovered that earning a paycheck was not the important thing. The whole point was to stand strong for those that couldn't do so for themselves. Although my insecurities of not having a job would resurface, I felt true inner peace. I realized that the great-est part of our humanity is when we cast aside our judgments and self- interest, not making ourselves the prime focus. Surrendering our will to the cause of another human being demands that we see their needs above our own — using *their* subjective measurement of hope and quality of life instead of our own.

Yes, just as a person confined to bed finds hope in eating his favorite food or seeing his grandchildren again, so does another find death the suitable option when artificial life support is the only means of sustaining that life. In order to truly live, we have to allow others do the same.

Redefining "Perfect"

If feelings of defeat and inadequacy arise, we must evaluate if we are throwing away our imperfect masterpieces or aspirations just because of our own pre-conceived perceptions or someone else's definition of the word "perfect." If this is the case, then we must redefine the term to fit our unique circumstances and abilities. If I had limited my first career choice to that of being a doctor, I would never have found the more conducive career as a social worker that I now enjoy. This alternative career choice has in no way diminished my dream of being in a profes-sion that would enable me to help others — one that meets both my physical and emotional needs.

I am not redefining the term "perfect" so that we can just lay back and take the easy way out, but to make it conducive to allow self-acceptance. And above all, make our dreams reality.

"Perfect" is not a one-size-fits-all term. We must be willing to customize it to our own life situation but this is easier said than done. It requires a willingness to redefine, not only a term, but ourselves. By redefining ourselves, we allow refining processes, life experiences, to mold and shape us into more than what we ever thought we could become. We do not judge ourselves on some broad abstract concept of normality or perfection that we have somehow ingrained within ourselves. We must discover everything that makes us who we genuinely are. Our disabilities and abilities are an integral part of the dynamic process of character building, and our acceptance makes up our individual wholeness. If the term "perfect" is redefined to include all of our perceived imperfections and differences, we have no excuse for not reasonably reaching our wholeness now — in the present moment.

Conclusion

Limitations should not provide excuses for passivity, but opportunities for full participation in building enduring foundations. It is imperative that we look beyond the perceived imperfections of our lives to discover what we are already perfectly capable of doing and being. It is only then that we will start to have moments and realizations that our imperfections and adversities, if we allow them, can be the very tools that assist us in becoming aware of our untapped potential, thereby transforming us into all we are meant to be.

Dormant strengths become active and moving forward is our only alternative. Cementing these seemingly "Majestic Moments" of realizations of truth into our lives completes our "Perfect Circle."

Men of vision caught glimpses of truth and beauty shining aloft like stars: and in these glimpses was a new hope for the unification of mankind through enlightenment.

—SIR ROBERT FALCONER

Chapter 2

Those Majestic Moments

JUST OUTSIDE LAS Vegas, Nevada, to the west next to the mountains, lies majestic Red Rock Canyon. Massive red sandstone rocks tower over the desert floor that look as if they had been sculpted by a skilled artisan. Desert flowers bloom in the spring, giving off shades of purple and yellow. I have always found refuge hiking the canyon trails. At one point in my life, the canyon symbolized something I most desired, an unchanging world or foundation. The mighty rocks always appeared to stand firm with unwavering confidence, unchanged by time or circumstance.

My desire was strongest when my own life circumstances appeared beyond my control, getting scarier and more treacherous with each passing moment. It was if I were on a roller coaster, hanging on with the whitest of knuckles. If only I could become one with the canyon and hug a rock. If so, I felt as if I could finally get off the scary ride and my life could be exactly what I expected it to be and on my terms.

As I have learned more about the geological processes of mother nature, the canyon doesn't remain unchanged, as I once had thought, but is dynamic and in constant flux and change. Millions of years have made the once underwater region into a dry desert. The elements of water, wind, and extreme heat have brought erosion that has made this magnificent landscape into what it is today: majestic. In another million years, when you and I are long gone, the canyon will take on yet a different look. New rock formations will rise; old ones will be reformed with the shifting of the earth. Different living habitats will evolve and perhaps others will become extinct.

These realizations have, for me, transformed the canyon from a refuge from change to a sanctuary for accepting change — the most fundamental of constants. Hugging such a "rock" would do little in my desperate quest for a static condition, as my once perceived unchanging friend would leave me far behind in its own progressive and changing journey to becoming an even more spectacular spectacle.

The canyon is just one example of how we can redefine ourselves as dynamic beings by allowing the hurdles or the inevitable forces of our lives to refine us. This can be a natural and healthy process for our betterment if we will quit standing in the way. Seeking an unchanging world is not only unrealistic, in every sense of the word, but it will invite strife and discontent into our lives as it cannot be halted — only resisted. The canyon, as beautiful as it is, offered me something equally as beautiful. I was given a glimpse of truth that would facilitate the realization that change is a natural process not to be feared or avoided, but embraced as one of the primary forces in our lives that promotes growth. This realization was, for me, as majestic as the scenes in the canyon, because it gave me the one insight or lesson I desperately needed at that particular time in my life. It was a moment of enlightenment or what I would term, a "Majestic Moment."

Moments of Bringing Truth Into Our Lives

THERE ARE MOMENTS of clarity when we suddenly discover that one nugget of truth about our human existence can bring to our minds majestic feelings of peace and serenity. These moments are a natural tranquilizer for the soul, taking away any uneasiness or anxiety, not because they necessarily answer all of our deepest questions, but because they offer a glimpse of truth that we need at a particular time in our life. Whether it's through our dreams, beholding a beautiful scene, silent prayer and meditation, or rendering acts of compassion, these glimpses of truth give us the inner assurance that we, too, are part of an enduring existence full of beauty and purpose. We must be the ones to decide to implement these sometimes small but profound nuggets of truth that are the "Majestic Moments" of our lives.

No matter what our beliefs are about the nature of the universe, these moments do not discriminate. We must not rationalize them away or dismiss them. Above all, we must accept the natural process of change and personal transformation. Though these moments sometimes require learning curves that may cause some discomfort, the pain is the awakening from outdated beliefs as the soul muscle is stretched, allowing truth to soar.

Allowing Truth to Soar

ONE OF MY favorite pastimes is to watch the big airliners land and take off at the airport runway. Since I can remember, I have been amazed by the fact that these large pieces of machinery can get off the ground — much less fly. During one of those times, I was also going through an introspective period in my life where I wanted to have all of life's deepest questions about the inner workings of the universe answered, once and for all. After all, I felt just as entitled to these exact answers as any of the great spiritual leaders had throughout the ages — or so I thought.

As I was watching a jumbo 747 taxi to get ready for take-off, a profound insight flashed through my mind. The thought came to me that although I have always liked to see planes fly, I knew very little of their mechanics or the laws of aerodynamics that govern flight. Then I thought, I didn't have to know all the technical matters in order to find enjoyment in seeing an airplane in action. In turn, my insight came that I don't need to know all the mysteries of the universe, with all of its wonders, to enjoy living in it. I only have limited knowledge of how our sun gives off warmth; but I still enjoy a bright sunny day. And so, at that "Majestic Moment," I had a glimpse of truth that I don't need to have all the answers, or know how everything I cannot see works, in order to embrace things like a loving universe with faith, hope, and prayer that summons its healing power to our unique needs. This insight left me with the lesson that I will always keep close by; that sometimes I dig too deep for the exact answers and go right past the truth!

What a paradox! In order to increase our capacity for understanding, we need to surrender our need to always understand. How wonderful it is that a 747 jet airplane can bring so much insight to one person.

Awakening to Reality

THERE ARE TIMES when every one of us has inflated our circumstances to such a proportion that ours lives appear overwhelming — like a runaway train. Sometimes we distort our reality by allowing life's smallest hurdles to ruin moments where everything is actually going quite well. We can't even enjoy the sunshine, because we are so fearful and anxious that a storm might appear! Then, when a storm does roll our way, we think it's personal, that we're the only ones in the cosmos facing such a disturbance. We feel singled out for trouble, when in reality, we aren't alone at all.

Yes, there are plenty of real storms or difficult periods in our lives, without having to create illusionary ones. I've created plenty of illusionary storms of my own, although I am now relieved to say I am getting considerably better in forecasting sunny days. I know as long as I'm human, I'll more than likely slip up occasionally, making, as the familiar saying goes, mountains out of molehills. But as with most of our experiences, there can be important lessons learned.

Making mountains in reality's landscape becomes an opportunity for a prompt evaluation to see if those mountains even remotely exist. The answer to a prayer concerning those "mountains" is solved the instant we start to put life's challenges into a perspective where they are not only seen as manageable, but as necessary tutorials for our long-term growth. The "big answer" we most often ignore comes when we suddenly understand that our obstacles are intended to be successfully worked through as an essential part of our life's experience — instead of as a justification for ruining our life. All we need to do is take the initiative to turn our mountains back to "molehills."

Reality Check

ONE MORNING, AS I was on my way to work, a storm was just passing over the valley where I live. It had been raining. There had been violent thunder and lightning the night before. The sun was finally peeking through and reflecting off the distant red rocks of the canyon with a crisp blue sky as the backdrop. The scene before me was not only beautiful, but significant.

That particular morning, I had knots in my stomach because of a conflict with one of my office co-workers. She had been refusing to talk and work with me for reasons that were, in the beginning, unknown. When I approached this person to see if there was any resolution or understanding that could be reached, she refused to talk about it. Every day was a struggle to come up with solutions to a problem that couldn't seem to be fixed. The most discomforting aspect of this entire situation was that I couldn't ignore her. In order to effectively do my job, I had to have clear and professional communication with her more than once a day. Every time I approached the department manager, he would order me to communicate with this person — using only e-mails. In fact, I was told if I failed to do this, disciplinary action would be taken against me with the possibility of termination at a company I had given everything to over the past six years. There I was, feeling totally threatened by a monster who had been at the company for less than a month. It seemed like she was going to eat me alive, with management supporting her cause. At that point, life seemed so unjust, and I was its victim, being isolated in a bubble with a dark cloud inside.

That particular day seemed especially dreadful, for some unknown reason, as conflict was something I always avoided, but was sure to confront. I desperately wanted the day to be perfect! Perfect in the way I perceived it, where everyone had a complete understanding of one another and got along. And, of course, where management would fix anything and we could all live happily ever after.

Thoughts kept screaming through my head. I questioned my self-worth and professional abilities, and all because someone had chosen not to associate with me. I was allowing another individual whom only a month earlier I didn't even know, much less care about what she thought, ruin a perfectly good day or days, and worse yet, my worth as a person. Just going to the office was like a death march. I was sure I'd have to pass that someone who was given permission to make me feel like someone less than I knew I was.

And who gave the permission? I did! I let another person disrupt my emotional well-being because of the belief I had somehow adopted that "everybody," regardless of the circumstances, should be able to understand and work well with one another. And of course, management should always make the right decisions, fixing everybody and everything in sight. I also carried the erroneous view that if things weren't this way, it was because I was physically disabled.

Two distinct profound truths came to me as I looked toward the canyon. First, I realized that as the beautiful rocks are not shaped and formed by static and calm conditions, so our lives can not always be as we expect or wish them to be. Part of our human condition is that people don't always have the amount of understanding or level of tolerance that we would want them to have. People who live and work together don't always see eye-to-eye or hold their perceptions in common, and those in management positions don't always have the expertise to fix the problem. But far more important is that none of us is being singled out to be put on life's chopping block. This is not to bring cynicism into the equation by saying that people are innately bad or evil, but instead, to enable us not to put our self-worth in jeopardy when people don't do the things or have the proper understanding as we would expect of them.

No, my uncomfortable work situation never got resolved the way I would have wanted. In fact, my cantankerous co-worker finally admitted, along with a few others who didn't enter my mind as having an issue with me, that she was very uncomfortable working alongside me because of my disability.

These weren't bad or uncaring people, and I'm sure that they had many good and admirable qualities. They were dealing with their own challenges of having to escape from their preconceived beliefs and insecurities that they had bought into over time about people who were physically different from themselves. Believe me, developing this perspective was not easy for me, especially when I was in the thick of it. At the time, I wanted them all to disappear. Looking back, these people were dealing with their own roadblocks to fully understanding others who were different than them. Why? Because they were also perfectly human! Just as I expected their understanding, I'm sure, whether or not they were aware of it, they expected mine. Breaking free from our limited perceptions of each other is a group project.

The second and equally important truth came into view as the distant scene of the canyon's own clearing storm brought me back into the reality — that the our life's storms eventually clear and the brightness of the light always returns. Then it dawned on me that although I had conflict at work with those whom I wanted to understand me, disability and all — at the moment of realization, there was absolutely nothing that would warrant disturbing either my physical or emotional well-being. I still had the ability to at least go to work and face my personal storms and that they would eventually clear. After all, what any person might think of me won't matter in another hundred years, and in all probability, a far shorter time than that.

That moment was, like the canyon in front of me, "majestic." It catapulted me back into the realization that what I thought at the time was a big storm was really nothing more than a little one, at best. And to take it one step further, as long as I had my health and those I loved and cared about had theirs, this couldn't be classified as an atmospheric disturbance — much less a storm.

Recognizing the profound truths in our lives comes when we have the ability to see through our illusions of self-created turmoil and come back to the reality that things are not really as bad as we have made them out to be. Our "Majestic Moments" can be a reality check when we realize we don't have to hold our self-worth hostage to another's perception of us. Just because we don't have mutual understandings from those we live and work with doesn't have to mean a storm is rolling in. And even if it does, we can know without doubt that it will soon pass. The true abundant life exists when the sky is full of black storm clouds and we can still see the brightness of the sun.

The Decision to Act

SOME OF THE most important and almost sacred moments in our lives are those when our thoughts become clear and the adversity is seen through the clearing ahead — all with the bright rays of strength, hope and an expanded perspective on whatever we are dealing. These are not eroding, but rather redefining opportunities that can build us a solid foundation that will withstand our storms and maintain our integrity. Often, we are oblivious to these moments until we introspectively look back on our lives as a panoramic picture, seeing how events and moments, even the painful ones, are the individual building blocks that build character to stand firm. The fleeting circumstances of life are allowed to change, and at times even knock us around, but who we are, with our courage, our hopes, and strengths propels us forward and becomes a standard fixture if we will stay the course.

Moments that potentially bring gifts of refinement are not once-in-a-lifetime events. As we become more aware of them, they come at every stage of our life. Being aware is not sufficient. We must consciously make a decision to act on our newly-discovered clarity. Once we wake up, it is imperative that we get up and do something before we go back to sleep. Once the alarm gently sounds, we cannot hit the snooze button. Whatever we call these experiences, be it enlightenment or "Majestic Moments," they may come to us while sitting far atop a mountain in a deep meditative state with our eyes shut or overlooking a serene mountain valley, but after a while, most of us will open our eyes and come down from the mountain and make the decision to act.

Instilling Worth in Others

ONE OF THE greatest acts of kindness and compassion we can offer each other is hope and worth — as a fellow human being. This is not done by exaggerated flattering remarks that we think are ego satisfying, but through unsolicited encouragement. It is in these times when lifting others up that we can feel as if we're answering our universal call to make a difference in the world. Even if we're just making a difference, one person at a time, this call is being successfully answered. It is then we realize that we truly are our brothers and sisters' keeper in the deepest sense. There is no greater philosophy of good will than, "Do unto others as you would have them do unto you."

Get Up Off the Floor

UP UNTIL THE ninth grade, I went to a school where all of my classmates were disabled. Growing up, I thought all kids my age had a physical disability of some kind. This was just a fact of life. My friends never thought anything about it when the teacher's aide would assist me or the other children in eating their lunch, nor did I think they cared as we all needed help with something. Nobody thought twice about what the other could or couldn't do because being disabled was the norm.

At recess, the favorite pastime was to play what we called "wheelchair war games." Those who could walk would take their best buddies that were in wheelchairs and push them around the playground. We would see how close we could get without hitting one another. Even though this was fun, there would always be a few visits a year to the nurse's office for accidents or the principal's office for not obeying the speed limit. This was our age of innocence. No one cared if we walked, talked a little different, or even had four wheels as legs. Getting to that playground to play our games seemed to be the only care any of us had at the time. Having a disability didn't seem to matter or be anything out of the ordinary.

The eighth grade came and went, and so did the age of innocence! In almost an instant, I became aware for the first time that I had a physical disability — that I was different than those with whom I shared my world. This sudden realization was devastating. I felt totally powerless over my future. I was in a body that I was sure would limit me in living life as I wanted. I felt as if I was surrounded by iron bars, in a body I had no other choice but to occupy. I had been born with a physical disability, but at this particular time in my life, I was just beginning to realize the full ramifications, or at least the ones running through my mind, of having to deal with a physical disability.

In 1975, a law was passed that would allow those with disabilities to attend the same schools as those without disabilities — or at least the noticeable disabilities. After all, we all have disabilities of one kind or another. Neither I nor my friends had any concept of what it would be like to attend a "different" school. Even though there were many changes, one thing would remain the same. We would still be riding the short bus that only carried the disabled kids. We had been riding this small bus for years and thought nothing of it. Like a limousine, we had door-to-door service. What may have seemed like a perk in having a disability now became another emotional hurdle.

As the short bus pulled onto the school campus, there would be hundreds of students racing around before the first bell rang. There were no wheelchairs or canes and everybody seemed to be walking unassisted. Some people would have to clear the way to make room for the small bus to drop us off. One select group of kids would always be waiting to pound on the bus, yelling, "cripples, retards." The real war began as the stark realization that I was different set in and the desire to be a part of the so-called normal world became etched into my psyche. Coming home after school and lying on my bed crying became routine. My only desire was to be somebody different than "what" I was. My mother would frequently look in on me in her own despair, feeling powerless to change a reality that only I could deal with. I remember lying awake at night, dreading the horror of humiliation that I knew I would experience the following day. Knots so tight they could snap developed in my stomach as every day we approached the same situation. I wanted to yell out to those kids, "I'm just like you! I just want to fit in!" I remember looking out the bus window and seeing all the kids who had, I thought at the time, what I didn't — a normal body. I wished so much that I could be transformed into one of them. At the time, I think I would have traded places with anybody: the geek, the football player, the guy with the purple mohawk — just to be able to fit in. I would have been virtually anybody — except who I was!

The emotional pain got so severe that as the bus pulled onto campus, I would get on the floor so as not to be seen. Bill the bus driver was understanding and would wait until most of the kids went inside before making me exit the bus. This avoidance behavior seemed to only mask the problem. The real pain remained my shame of being different.

One morning, when I was crouched on the floor of the bus, Bill provided me encouragement that would help me begin to change how I would see myself and others. He stopped the bus, turned around, looked straight down at me and said, "John, you're just as good or maybe even better than any of those kids out there! Stand up! Be confident and make some friends! And remember, not everyone is going to like you. That's just life."

These challenging remarks of encouragement triggered the insight or "Majestic Moment" that would plant a seed to a more expansive view of who I really was. This made it possible for me to start down my path of self-acceptance.

The bus driver's encouragement didn't act like a magic wand, making me into the most emotionally secure human being on planet earth, instantly popular and self-confident. But it did trigger the moment when insight came that I needed to get up off the floor of that bus and start to accept my life and its challenges. After all, like it or not, you can't move forward when you're lying down!

The words, "that's just life" remains echoing through the forefront of my mind, not as a cue to just roll over and take what life dishes out, but to accept what is and then find a way to move beyond. It was at that moment I absolutely knew it was up to me to decide whether or not to take action on this insight that had the potential to change my entire outlook on life. My self-esteem gradually grew as I took the action that would start my journey out of self-pity. A week or two later, I let others see me get off that short bus — disability and all.

At first this was so difficult to do. Each day I had to resist the temptation to get back on the bus floor by keeping the bus driver's words of encouragement running through my mind. I had to stand up for myself! No matter how emotionally painful, it was my only alternative. Eventually, I realized there were only a couple of inconsiderate kids who were calling me names. It dawned on me that the rest of the student body might possibly be willing to accept me as a friend — if only I would give "them" a chance. Little did I know that at that stage in my life, I needed to accept myself before I could be accepted by others.

Being Ourselves

LEARNING TO BE comfortable with myself turned into a series of very uncomfortable wake-up calls — leading to the freedom of self-acceptance. At first, I thought that everyone without a physical disability must have an existence that was problem free. Getting enough courage to get off the floor of the bus was just the first step in building my self-esteem and confidence. The next step was to realize that my physical differences didn't make me special or out of the ordinary, but rather, someone who was only human. Unfortunately, in our adolescent years, these thoughts can't be fully realized because they are merely in their infancy of being formed.

Our adolescence, and in most cases even our early adult years, are the most difficult time periods in the rite of passage into genuine self-acceptance. And this process will continue throughout our entire life!

It is during these years that we seek an identity. This difficult process is where we begin wanting to emulate those we admire in order to find our true selves. Instead of looking within to discover who we really are, we look outward, wanting to be something or someone we're not, ever can be, or ought to be. The illusion that other people are somehow better off, with absolutely no problems or adversities of their own, sets us up for frustration, because we see ourselves singled out as the only ones having to deal with life's most difficult challenges. One of the most important insights we can make about ourselves is conquering the challenge of finding our personal wholeness and the willingness to be ourselves. With this willingness we cannot help but discover our hero within.

The Hero Within

As I was going through this difficult growing process, I vividly recall walking through the hallways of my high school thinking I was the only one who was worried about acceptance and "fitting in." I remember thinking that if I could be like the coolest and most popular person on campus, I would be totally complete and never want anything — ever again! Knowing that I could never be such a person, I looked outward to fulfill this need.

One day, while sitting alone and isolated in the lunch room, Joe, one of the most popular people at school, introduced himself to me. I had always known this particular person to have everything I thought I wanted out of life. He had good looks and every girl on campus wanted to be his girlfriend! He was the football quarterback, and to top it off, he drove a motorcycle.

Joe did the incomprehensible! Though I felt undeserving that anybody of this stature would extend his hand in friendship to me — he did! In retrospect, I have no idea what gave Joe the motivation to take the time, effort, and perhaps courage to befriend someone who appeared so outwardly different than he. After all, he had all the friends one would ever need. All I do know is that by doing so, he gave me something I craved at that time in my life, acceptance from others, a gift I cherish today. Throughout my junior and senior years, I rode to and from school on the back of his motorcycle. No longer did I perceive myself as that poor little disabled boy on the floor of the short school bus, but someone who was on the road to acceptance among his peers.

Unfortunately, this perceived sense of security ended when Joe left my side. My sense of worth depended on someone being present outside of me. If Joe was absent, so was my new found sense of self-worth.

After graduating from high school, Joe moved away and I did not hear from him until ten years later when I received an unexpected call. He was passing through town and wanted to see me.

The person who showed up at my door was not the cool guy I wanted to be like in my adolescence, but instead, someone I hoped never to allow myself to become. Joe showed up that day looking to be in a poor state of health. He proceeded to tell me he was just having a fun time in Las Vegas with some of his buddies. He said they all had been awake for five straight days doing cocaine.

Not only did I not want to be like him, I felt very uncomfortable having him in my home as he and his buddies felt at liberty to do their illegal drugs right in front of me. I felt compelled to ask them to leave after a brief visit.

As he left, Joe pulled me aside to tell me that as I had once looked up to him, he now looked up to me! His life was in shambles — literally destroyed by drug and alcohol abuse. He seemed ashamed that he had wasted a good part of his life on those things that were destroying him.

I have not seen or heard from Joe since that last visit. I sincerely hope he has found the strength within himself to improve his life, moving in a positive direction. As for my own life, this experience has afforded me the profound realization that we can not find true self-worth through other things or people.

Our "Perfect Circle" can only successfully be completed by ourselves. No one can do it for us. Only we can pick ourselves up from the floor of the bus. The downside to this rather unpleasant reality is that we have to do the work while the upside is we are the captains of our own vessels. The opportunity of meeting Joe later in life had given me the profound insight that having the perfect body, being quarterback, or driving a motorcycle does not exempt one from his own hurdles. No matter how much better off another may appear, the truth of the matter is that every last one of us has to deal with challenges and adversities that are unique to each individual. Some problems are better disguised than others, but the reality is if we are perfectly human, we all have problems. We can all have heroes or people we look up to for encouragement as long as we first and foremost look up to the only one that can truly come to our rescue, the hero within!

Conclusion

WE'VE ALL HAD our short bus stories or times when it was difficult to believe in ourselves or adjust to not being able to perfectly fit into the mold we think is the norm. It is in these difficult times that we can either test the strength of our foundations, build upon them, and make them even stronger, or we can allow them to tear us down. The choice is ours!

These difficult times are the personal storms that bring those refining "Majestic Moments" in which the seeds of inspiration must be nourished — both individually and collectively. These moments of truth that flow into our lives facilitate the refreshing realization that we wouldn't trade our life with another — as my own, and hopefully yours, has ultimately turned out perfect for our individual growth. Throughout this book, these refining "Majestic Moments" will be referred to as they are intertwined into life's tapestry to trigger our continued growth.

*Although the world is full of suffering,
it is also full of the overcoming of it.*
—HELEN KELLER

Chapter 3

How Far Down is Up?

I RECALL ONCE when the 6 o'clock evening news forecast rain and wind for the following day. The weatherman made a public apology stating, "Unfortunately, there's rain and wind in tomorrow's forecasts, but don't worry; hopefully, the sun will be out later this week." The odd thing about this reluctant forecast was that the western half of the United States had been experiencing a five-year drought and rain was desperately needed. So the stormy weather should have been welcomed instead of pushed away as bad news. Sunny and clear days are always great and we should embrace them with open arms, but the fact is that we need cloudy, rainy days to replenish our water supply and to provide nourishment to the beautiful needful things of our earth. And so it is with our personal lives.

Our Inner Navigational System

THE SEEDS OF our greatest potential are given nourishment through our personal stormy days. Feelings of hopelessness and despair leading to the epidemic of depression are not desired emotions. But in many cases, these feelings act as our inner compass that can warn us when a change of direction is needed — especially if what we are currently doing is tearing us down instead of building us up. We may call this compass by any term we wish as long as we are able to acknowledge that every one of us has an inner navigational system. The purpose of this system is to guide us toward growth that enables us to reach our highest potential. We've all heard people say, "I've hit bottom" or "I'm sick and tired of being sick and tired." These statements are made when one is at the bottom of his personal pit. Hopefully, an overriding desire to start making positive changes is close at hand.

In many cases, illegal drug and alcohol use, or other less noticeable behaviors such as working excessively or having co-dependent relationships with people or things are used as a means to avoid dealing with the real issues. It can seem easier to numb the discomfort of low self-worth with the use of drugs and alcohol, thus avoiding the real changes we need to make to move upward. Addictive behaviors suppress the call that we need to move in an alternative direction. This masquerading only deepens our pit, leaving the bottom and positive change further from our sight. The seriousness of these behaviors can lead to hospitalization, or if left unattended, even suicide.

It is vital that we learn how to read or feel our inner compass and then move in a positive direction, making the needed changes to our lives. Old or outdated support systems must be dropped to make room for ones that will be supportive of our decision to climb out of our rut. Sometimes seeking outside professional support from a physician, therapist, or treatment program may be a necessary first step toward constructive change.

An Overriding Desire

MY FIRST JOB out of college as a social worker was working at a small drug and alcohol treatment facility. This residential facility was exclusively designed to treat women with young children. The children were allowed to live with their mothers under court-ordered child protective supervision on the condition that the treatment program was successfully completed. It appeared that most of the residents had a history of being in and out of various drug and alcohol treatment programs for years — with little to no success. However, I did see a few women who had successfully gotten their addiction under control. They were able to lead healthy productive lives in society with their families. Some even became certified counselors and later worked in a professional capacity at the same facility where they had once been treated for their own addictions.

In getting to know them, I found the secret of their success — an overriding desire to vacate the world of uncontrolled addiction and get their lives back. They were the ones who, after not paying attention to their internal compass and patterns of destructive behavior, finally got to the point where an upward direction was not only desired, but self-mandated.

Even though I had earned my master's degree and was state certified and licensed, these counselors, who had experienced the pit of addiction themselves, were the real teachers of how upward movement to reach one's highest potential could become reality. Even though they were all unique, they all expressed the common theme that their success came as a result of hitting bottom and then having the overriding desire to bounce up. They all were sick and tired of having a substance control their lives, always having to be under the watchful eye of the law. They were on the streets or in abusive relationships or both, revolving in and out of different court-ordered treatment programs, and, most of all, being under the illusion of freedom while never actually having it. All of them were able to express that their "bottom of the pit" was clearly in focus and the only alternative was to either die or take a proactive stance toward positive change. The path they chose was obvious and I was privileged to not only work alongside them, but to learn from them the valuable lesson — that real change is difficult but possible.

It was amazing to hear they all had that one moment in their lives where realizations surfaced and their perspective went from a world of confinement to one where their true potential was in sight. These heroic individuals discovered that the sun really does shine again after the passing storm. They are a true example that the transforming power to positively change our lives is within reach of us all.

Addicted to Victimhood

OFTEN OUR PERSONAL storms begin when we take the position that life has handed us more than we can bear and it's unfair. We have all gone through these periods; it's a natural cycle where we feel the world is against us. We feel we're the only ones being singled out to take life's beatings, while everyone else around us is getting off scot-free with no challenges of their own to work through. When we think the weekly talk show guests are having a smoother life than we are, we need to take a little self-inventory to see how far down we really are in our personal pit, dug by the shovel of "victimhood."

Our long-term vision and perspective is clouded by what appears to be a series of insurmountable roadblocks that we feel absolutely powerless to remove. As with healing and flushing our bodies of damaging impurities from a virus, thereby strengthening our physical immune system, so do short periods of feeling helpless and hopeless strengthen the resiliency of the human spirit. It's when we're pushed into a corner, feeling like a trapped victim or hitting the bottom of our personal pit of self pity that we allow our emotional immune system, or human spirit, to prompt us to take action. Answers to the empowering question, "What can I do about it?" start to manifest. Sudden flashes of ideas and inspiration flood our minds on how we can rise above it all. Roadblocks are cut down to size and even disappear, and we begin to recognize ways to transform these painful periods of our lives into a valuable curriculum for personal growth.

Emerging from the pit of victimhood is not always easy. It takes perseverance. It is the inner workout that ultimately manifests itself outwardly in our actions. We all have the opportunity to stretch ourselves and realize that although we can't always fix our external circumstances, we can still view them in a way that can allow us to rebound from our personal pit — higher than we ever thought we could. We need to stop comparing ourselves to the abilities of others and see the potential for our own growth. Instead of seeing a physical disability as an unfair hindrance, we see it as an opportunity to connect; having a heightened awareness and empathy for others we could not have had any other way. We gain a better understanding of the power of the human spirit to assist us in transcending those things we cannot change by seeing them in a different light and then extending this hope to others. We take on the role of both teacher and student in the course of overcoming, instead of settling for, victimhood. We feel alive again because of our decision to move forward and change our point of view.

The detrimental question of the day is, "why me?" The more desperate we are to come up with a valid answer to this ageless question, the more victimized and hopeless we become. The question can only be answered by the ego, the very real and necessary part of us that takes the "fight or flight" response. The ego is useful when we're in a situation where we need to respond fast for our survival, but it can be detrimental when an expansion of our perspective is needed. Take it from me, someone who in the past asked the "why me" question plenty of times, only to receive the shallow answer, "because you're a victim and life's treating you unfairly."

Asking our ego such a question delays finding the deep and meaningful answers that enables us to have the capability to gain wisdom and inner strength through whatever we are experiencing. Instead of asking "why me?" we should be asking the alternative question, "why not me?" And then, "what can I do about it?" Both of these questions have a healing effect on the soul as they beg an answer from the inner technology of the human spirit that sees our life from a grander perspective.

If we fail to reconfigure from feeling like the victim, using our thoughts and actions as a catalyst for positive change, we will entrap ourselves in a stagnant, or worse yet, downward spiral. We will be left trying to flee from what appears to be a dangerous situation, instead of one where all that is required is to creatively adapt and see things differently. As with all addictions, people and situations will come out of the woodwork to validate our belief of hopelessness. They will often encourage us to accessorize ourselves in the by-products of addiction that come in the dismal packaging of cynicism, backbiting, gossip and most noticeably, non-acceptance of anything and everything.

Let's not forget the other harmful addictions, like substance abuse, can control us by numbing our emotions that are the warning signs we're digging a deeper pit for ourselves. What can we do to make our feelings of being the victim become part of our "Perfect Circle" — thereby using them to make us stronger? Bouncing up and out of the pit mandates surrendering to a process that, however difficult in initiating, will be worth the effort. And what is this process? Simply stated, we make the human spirit the pilot, and relegate the ego to co-pilot, assisting us in those situations where "fight or flight" emergency signaling is needed.

Bouncing Up

I'VE HAD OTHER personal storms of my own. The most notable occurred after graduating from high school and coming to the stark realization that I would now have to make my own choices. Would I give in to my physical limitations or rise above them? My parents and loving grandparents always instilled in my mind the expansive view that I could do and be anything I wanted, with the minor exception of a brain surgeon. But there were still those around me, with a limited view, who coached and advised me to let my parents or the state take care of me. After all, I was just a victim of an unfortunate circumstance.

Even though this was not what I wanted out of life, it seemed my only alternative at this point. Although all these people were well-intentioned in offering their perspective, for me it was like a destructive drug. If taken frequently, this drug would enable me to play the victim, a role that I learned to play exceptionally well by seeing random unfairness dealt from life's deck of cards.

There were those whose opinions I valued, who suggested that panhandling on the Las Vegas Strip to be the only suitable occupation for me to gain the autonomy I sought. Like someone who is brought down by drugs or alcohol, so was I if I chose to be the victim. However, despite my good health and a wide range of opportunities, I chose not to give any of the positive aspects of my reality any of my energy whatsoever. At this stage in my life and development, I found it quite gratifying to be addicted to the helpless destructive drug of "victim-hood" instead of taking charge of my life and creatively adapting my disabilities to my challenges so I could start moving forward.

That addiction was so strong that it blinded me to any positive input from my own family or friends and I gravitated toward nega-tivity and those who were feeding that self-destructive path. After all, the people who genuinely love us the most don't have a handle on what's real or good for us, or so the addicted person would like to reason. We are often blinded to the bright rays of hope shining through the dark storm clouds that are merely passing. And, just like a person addicted to drugs or alcohol, I justified my use and abuse of victimhood with my personal view that life was unfair. The question of the day became, "why me?" instead of, "why not me?" Or better yet, "what can I do about it?"

Life teaches us the difficult lesson of taking responsibility for our own thoughts and actions. Others can encourage us, but ultimately, no one can make us become something we have no desire of becoming.

We have to see the possibilities, sooner rather than later, before we dig too deep into our own pit of victimhood. My life became a downward spiral when I played the victim role over an extended period of time. I actually did start drinking excessive amounts of alcohol in order to numb my emotional pain of feeling helpless and, above all, hopeless. It was that one moment of personal introspection and insight or the "Majestic Moment," where I realized that I hit bottom and was sick and tired of assuming the role of the helpless, disabled victim.

I had all the external support I would need to move forward. My parents believed in me. They were willing to pay for my college education so that I could become whatever I wanted to become in life. But more importantly, I had to offer myself internal support. I had to believe in myself and stop listening and feeding off the negative destructive drug dealers that were enabling my hopelessness. No matter how many self-help bestsellers I read, I could not find the one quick-fix answer to my emotional crisis. Ultimately, I had to decide to take proactive action to fix anything that had to do with "me." No amount of people or words written in a book could come to my rescue. Only I could be the one to rescue myself. This realization, though startling, was my most important step forward. It was at that point I decided to begin the upward ascent out of the hole that I had dug with the "why me?" shovel and replaced it with, "what can I do about it?"

After this affirmative decision was made, giving me a new purpose in life, I enrolled in college to get my undergraduate degree in political science. I graduated and completed my master's in social work. At first, my upward climb was extremely difficult. Outdated thoughts that had accumulated over the years, conditioning me to be the helpless victim, had to be replaced with more innovative ones that would enable me to move toward my new horizon. Each day became a challenge, while facing the temptation to again travel the road that would lead me back down to where I had already been.

Once I made the decision to attend college and get off my pity-pot, new roads appeared almost overnight to pave the way to a new upward direction. I now had the option to choose between two roads, one that led backwards, and the other forward. I now had the vision of what I could become, if I so desired. My self-determination and positive attitude were at an all-time high. No one would just hand me a college degree or more importantly, my self worth. I had to earn them both!

Although it is encouraging to have others believe in us, it will do little good, unless we believe in ourselves. I had to be the one to decide to abandon old thought patterns and adopt new ones, and then take the appropriate action.

I vividly recall the tightness in my stomach on my first day as a college freshman. At the time, it all seemed so overwhelming and intimidating. Fears of not being accepted and fitting-in resurfaced. My mind traveled back to when I was in high school. All the same feelings and the accompanying emotions resurfaced. I had to realize that these fears were outdated and no longer applied to me. I had no need to hold on to them because I had moved on in my life. Now was the time to see myself as someone who was more confident and ready to take responsibility for his future.

This transformation process required stepping into the unknown, embracing uncertainty to take on new roles that would, at times, be very uncomfortable. Stepping out of the victim role meant taking the risk of not succeeding on the first try, at moving forward; and, at meeting my own expectations.

I found the risk to be well worth the discomfort — because if I didn't, I would still be lying on the floor of that short bus. I allowed myself to experience discomfort as I continued to move forward with my life. And with time, the picture I had of myself gradually changed to accommodate the new challenges ahead. The great thing about feeling fear and moving beyond it anyway, is that we not only have the opportunity to bounce back, but also bounce higher than we ever thought we could.

Maintaining the Momentum

WE CAN BE sure that life will always throw a curve ball our way and the possibility of a downward spiral will resurface. Just when we think we have won the race, there's still more road to be traveled and there must be an awareness that a conscious upward momentum still needs to be maintained. We must realize, since life always wants us to be in a constant growth mode, that life's pertinent lessons will always keep coming our way.

I have frequently asked myself if there will ever be a time I reach a point when I will have mastered the art of living — making the rest of my life a free-sailing experience. Frankly, sometimes I think this would be quite nice. The answer to this question has always come through loud and clear, that the flow of growth opportunity experiences never stop confronting us while on our path to greater potential. Even when we feel as if we've conquered the world, we should always expect there is still something more from which we can learn and grow. If one day we can say with confidence that we truly believe in ourselves and our abilities, we should expect and welcome people and situations coming our way to test the accuracy of this knowledge. Outdated thoughts and insecurities that make their way back into our experience are the curve balls that are thrown our way to see if we will successfully hit them and make that home run. Just when we think the feelings associated with prior fears and insecurities will never again return, situations come our way that tempt us to return to previously unproductive scripts and roles.

The Curve Ball

WHEN I GRADUATED with my master's degree in social work, I was confident that my first resume would be eagerly welcomed and I would rapidly find my first job out of college. After all, my school intern supervisor had not only given me high marks on my performance evaluations, but had also assured me that my disability actually added to my professional credibility by being able to more fully emotionally connect with my clients. I knew without a shadow of a doubt that any insecurity I once had was flushed away and never to be seen again. Boy, was I off the mark! Big time!

My first job interview was at a rehabilitation hospital. Not only would I be doing the exact job that I had previously done with high marks during my college internship, but I also had a friend at that hospital, who was the director of social services. I was sure that she would "juice me in." After all, I lived in Las Vegas!

I went to my first job interview as confident as anybody could be — dressed for success and ready to step into my new career. To the interview, I brought letters of reference and a resume that I thought would captivate any audience. I believed that my prior professional experiences would surely be impressive. I already had two years of interning at a rehab hospital just like the one at which I was currently interviewing. In addition, I had two years experience as a sensitivity speaker for the human resource department at the new MGM Grand Hotel in Las Vegas. All this was certainly more than enough to not only make me a prime candidate for the job — but the only candidate!

As I was walking to the car after the interview, my ego took a beating as my friend, who I thought could make this job a shoo-in, came out to speak with me. She compassionately put her arm around me and in confidence broke the bad news that the people conducting the interview had already made up their mind that they would not hire a disabled person to fill the social work position. At that moment, I felt I had just been told I had a terminal disease. I again felt my old helpless emotions enclose around me — like a shock wave. I went home discouraged, ready to resume my victimhood role. I felt as if all my education and training efforts had been in vain. There I was, feeling like an unemployable disabled victim.

I immediately contacted the vocational rehabilitation department to get further guidance on how to get employment as a disabled person. I now realized that I may need additional help in breaking into the professional world. They made me an appointment for an initial consultation and later, I met with the vocational rehab counselor.

I had hope as the counselor assigned to my case was not only legally blind and in a wheelchair, but he also had his master's in social work. He would surely be able to empathize with my situation. After completing his intake assessment, the counselor took a week to review his workup. On my next appointment, he called me in and in a matter of fact way told me my disability was so severe that as a social worker, I was unemployable! He then advised me to apply for disability assistance through Social Security as a means of getting financial support for the rest of my life.

There is absolutely nothing wrong with these programs for those who really need them. But I had six years of post high-school education, earning both a bachelor's and master's degree. I had already proven I could do the job at a prior internship position. Now I felt that I really had an excuse to be the victim — since the person telling me I was unemployable because of my disability was himself disabled.

No matter how well-intentioned this vocational rehab counselor may have been, I realized at that discouraging moment, only I knew the truth about myself. I was employable and if only I knew it, then so be it! If I didn't believe in myself, then who could? I was so determined to prove this reality that I sent out resume after resume. I pounded the pavement and met everyone, anyone, who would listen and offer me employment. I needed to know and make true what I knew to be true — to manifest itself into reality.

The daily challenge that confronted me was to not backslide into the role of being the helpless victim. I couldn't let negative self-talk drag me back down to where I had already been. I had to affirm and reaffirm the belief that I was moving forward and this had to be my new reality with no other alternatives.

Within a six-month period, I went to more than thirty-four job interviews. All with no success! I gave myself no alternative but to hang on and achieve what I wanted and knew I deserved. Every potential employer indicated that they would require me to have at least one year of job experience before even considering me for a position. All of them felt that a prior college internship did not satisfy this requirement. Now I felt I had two strikes against me. I was not only disabled, but I also had no prior paid job experience! I had to first get a job to find one.

Close to the brink of giving up, I finally came across a job offer for a case management position at a small substance abuse treatment facility. I went to the interview and was offered my first job — at $8.50 an hour and full healthcare benefits. I accepted the job, knowing that it was another positive step toward a successful social work career.

I stayed at this job for one year, until I was able to eventually move on to a higher paying position. The process became easier and easier as time passed and I professionally advanced. With each step came new abilities, and above all, confidence! I reaffirmed to myself the belief that anything I set out to achieve, with concentrated effort, would ultimately pay off. Often we miss out on the payoff because we discount it as something less than we expected. We need to have the patience and above all, faith, for all the things that are working together to our benefit — unfolding in their own "perfect" time. In retrospect, taking my first post-masters professional position at the low hourly rate was not settling for less, as some had thought, but a position that helped me gain the experience, confidence, and momentum to make my dream into reality.

Even today, I continue to be confronted by people and situations that force me to wonder if I'm still choosing to play the role of the helpless disabled victim. And when I find myself slipping back into those outdated thoughts and behaviors, I now take a few steps back, embrace what I need to learn, apply what I already have, and then move forward from there. The amazing thing about life is that it will always give us ample opportunities, or curve balls, to take a self-inventory and provide windows for an inner tune-up to make sure we have the capability to successfully maintain the momentum to successfully travel the road ahead.

More often than not, anything worth achieving comes with a price! And that price is persistent diligent effort when we're up, and more importantly, those times when we're down! The down times in our lives are when we need to concentrate our efforts to find creative solutions to our circumstances — instead of throwing in the towel.

Passing on Perseverance

OUR FAMILIES, AND those we are close to, pass on their perseverance legacy to us. One of the greatest benefits of our relationships is the "building effect" they have on our individual lives. Grandparents tell of how they lived through the Great Depression of 1929, surviving on less material things while still making ends meet. An applicable lesson for all generations!

Parents relay their successes and even failures in hopes that they either will or will not be repeated by their children. Our family members and those we love cannot carry us through life, but they can instill within us some passion and words of wisdom to carry along our journey.

Teachers aren't required to live problem-free lives, as they, too, are "imperfectly" human. And if they aren't, their teaching credentials are flawed. If we don't have family and loved ones to gain wisdom from, we can open up the possibility that those we share the planet with can be counted as our extended family. Kinship is not just because of bloodline, but can also be felt because we all share one common denominator — traveling life's sometimes down and then back-up journey. While others cannot go through life for us, they can certainly provide us with some excellent pointers. Just like the passing of the Olympic torch, so, too, will earlier generations pass on their wisdom, experience, and perseverance to each of us.

Passing the Torch

MY FATHER HAS been yet another prime example to me, and those who know him, of how persistent diligent effort is definitely worth the price and always pays off in the end. Since I can remember, he has always worked hard to create success around him — even when times and circumstances got rough.

He always seemed to quickly lift his spirits up when he was down. He only saw opportunities ahead. Hurdles were meant to be stepped over with the sure and confident knowledge of that which lies ahead is far greater than what we left behind. For him, every battle is but part of the upward journey. And at times, I actually saw him get a great deal of excitement in fighting the battle.

I have to admit that when I went to him in my times of despair and discouragement, I would sometimes feel as if he was uncaring and calloused. He would tell me that to succeed in life, I must keep my head high and creatively adapt and forget about all the rest. I used to think during my "victim" periods that this advice only worked if you were in a high profile business position like he was, but not someone who was lowly and physically disabled like me. But as I matured, I realized that my father was building within me all the self-confidence and faith that was needed to move upward when I was down or thought I'd hit bottom. For him, to forget the rest meant to leave behind the negative and start focusing on the positive! These weren't just idle words, but a philosophy my father has successfully demonstrated throughout his life.

One such demonstration of my father's positive philosophy began in 1980, when my father created a million dollar laser-light and dueling robot show for the 1981 Knoxville World's Fair.

He had spent long and hard days to not only create the high tech extravaganza, but to guarantee its placement in an entertainment venue that would be sure to prove its success. Nevertheless, all negotiations fell through for the World's Fair, even though the investor's money was spent and over a million dollars in hardware was sitting dormant.

I remember my father immediately getting on the telephone to make alternative plans for his creation. His laser-light and dueling robot show known as "Euphoria" was redesigned to be portable so that it could travel the state and county fair circuit. It promised to be the first traveling Disney-type attraction to be at a fair or theme park. The show made its debut with the anticipation of drawing crowds and robust revenues. When the first show was to begin, the sophisticated highly technical equipment kept shutting down and the patrons demanded refunds for their tickets. Soon he discovered that the fairground dusty environment was not conducive to the high-tech equipment and the set-up and operating expense far outweighed expected revenue — even if the show was perfectly run.

As the days wore on, the technical problems could not be resolved. Thousands of dollars were lost, and the investors started coming to my father for answers of why his project was not working and generating revenues he had promised. Fair after fair came and went with the same results. Hundreds of thousands of dollars were lost with zero profit. Never before had I seen my father in such despair. For the first time in my life, I heard him say how hopeless he felt with no light in sight at the end of the tunnel.

It was not long after the moment I saw my father hit the bottom of his personal pit that I saw him start to bounce back by planning a trip to Las Vegas. His goal was to create the ultimate impersonator production show.

His creative mind integrated look-a-like superstars like Elvis Presley, Marilyn Monroe, and many others, with his high-tech laser-lights and other exotic special effects. His seed has sprouted into the longest-running Las Vegas Strip production show! It all began in 1983.

That once small seed grew into the world-renowned stage show, *Legends in Concert*. That show has been entertaining audiences as it has traveled the globe. On Stage Productions was later formed into a multi-million dollar publicly traded company that my father would later resign from as chairman of the board. He did that in order to expand his own opportunities and possibilities even more.

For him, it was time to move on from the very company he created in order to capture the totality of the vision he held for himself. He went on to have a New York Broadway show.

My father now credits his success to what he refers to as the "Euphoria Experience" — an experience that took him all the way to the bottom of his personal pit of despair and hopelessness, and left him with what seemed to be nothing. But as he looks back, he sees this same experience as his refinement process. It enabled him to better navigate within his professional world, as he has climbed the ladder of success with a more solid foundation and understanding of his own ability and confidence.

I've adopted his "Euphoria Experience." It keeps me believing that my life's down times are really opportunities in disguise for growth and a heightened awareness of the ever-expanding potential that is within each one of us. My father may never know how much he has inspired me with his life, just as we may never know how much we inspire each other with our own. He has taught me the value of moving on with life, leaving behind the past while learning from it as we move forward to greater possibilities. The counsel that he gave me in my own periods of "being down" was just the antidote I needed. I have come to realize that sometimes the flowery touchy-feely words of encouragement are not always what are needed to lift us up. Sometimes we need to hear my father's hard-hitting words of encouragement as he would tell each of us to keep our head high, creatively adapt and keep moving in a positive direction as we take the torch.

Conclusion

The 1989 movie, *Parenthood*, starring Steve Martin, concerned the day–to-day trials and tribulations of raising a family. The elderly grandmother, one of the movie's delightful characters, makes a most profound and insightful analogy in teaching the important lesson of embracing both the up and down times of our life's journey. She does this by comparing a merry-go-around with a roller coaster.

She teaches us that the merry-go-around is boring. It just goes around and around, while the roller coaster is exciting. It goes up and down and takes your stomach in the process. She continues to make a clear statement for each one of us to remember: that life is to be lived to the fullest, as she prefers the roller coaster, with all of its ups and downs, hanging on with the belief that each downward angle will soon lead upward.

This does not mean we should always expect to be screaming with laughter and excitement. There will inevitably be times in our lives when we scream in or with pain — be it physical, emotional, or both! We may cry in times of loss or just search in desperation for some kind of meaning to life. When these times come, we can hang on with confidence, with the inner assurance that we did not let one life experience go past us without learning something more about the resiliency of the human spirit.

So, go ahead and board life's roller coaster!

To nourish the soul means to participate in the very mechanics of creation — to become a co-creator of your life and of the world as you want it to be.

—WAYNE DYER

Chapter 4

Holding the Vision

I'VE ALWAYS ENJOYED talking about the life experiences and observations of those who are older than I. What is the most amazing is *their* amazement at the last century's progressive technological advances. Such modern conveniences as the airplane, automobile, and television have evolved from mere seeds that were only visions of great minds. My grandmother recalled an exciting childhood event when a biplane landed in the school yard of her one-room schoolhouse. She further recalled that since neither she nor any of her schoolmates had ever seen an actual airplane before, they all ran out in excitement to see the flying marvel come in for a landing.

Her experience made me realize individuals like the Wright brothers, who first envisioned a machine that could actually fly, have impacted how succeeding generations saw their world. The Wright brothers had the courage to explore the laws of aerodynamics enough not only to bring their vision into focus, but into everyday reality for you and me to make travel easier. Today, their one seed has grown into a technology that can transport us to the other side of the world in a matter of hours.

What if these visionary brothers had believed in the opinions and narrow mindedness of others — that flight was not possible? It is through the conviction and courage of great visionaries that realities are formed and solidified. Greatness is formed when we say, "never say never" to our dreams and aspirations, thereby allowing our planted seeds to take their charted course, growing and ultimately taking flight.

Holding the Collective Vision

AS WE LOOK back on our individual life stories, we can't help but find people who were instrumental in facilitating the discovery process of our potential. While we ultimately are responsible for nurturing our own visions and aspirations, it is these key individuals we can look back on and say that without their encouragement and influence at pivotal points in our lives, we would not be where we are today. Whether it's our parents who had the vision of bringing us into the world, a childhood teacher who chose to spend extra time with us, or the bus driver, these are the people who hold a vision for us as we strive to get our own bearings and stay the course. During pivotal times in ours lives, the power of many is imperative to propel us successfully into our solo journey.

The Power of Many

AS MY PARENTS were anticipating my birth, preparations were being made for the new nursery. My mother vividly recalls feeling the excitement for the new addition to her family. The day, March 1, 1966, arrived and my mother gave birth and started me on my life's journey. A day that was intended for anticipation and excitement quickly turned to a day my father describes as the worst day of his life.

The doctor came to the waiting room to reluctantly tell him there had been delivery complications. I was without oxygen for four minutes that had caused irreparable damage to the region of my brain that controls my body's motor functions. At first, the doctors only gave me a few days to live. The grim news almost shattered my parents' dreams of having their first son. My father recalls that he was so devastated and angry that he went home and tipped over every piece of furniture in the nursery. Knowing that he needed to draw on a power greater than himself, he recalled his anger and despair and turned to hope and faith as he got on his knees to pray for a future that included me. He describes how he began to have an inner feeling that not only would I live, but that I would be able to live a healthy productive life.

Clergy and family members came to the hospital to offer their collective prayers on my behalf. The next morning, the doctors came with encouraging news that I would live, but that I would be severely physically and perhaps mentally disabled — never to be able to walk or talk or live without constant care. The medical experts assured my parents that I would never be a productive human being.

Prayers continued for a miracle, overturning this grim prognosis. Even after being diagnosed with cerebral palsy, those who loved me held me in their vision as someone who was constantly improving, gaining more ability every day to live a more fulfilling life. My mother took me to physical therapy three days a week. This support was backed by her constant faith in my steady improvement. My loving family's mission was to diligently teach me to do those things that the doctors told my parents I would never be able to do.

It was the collective power of love that taught me to walk — which I eventually did learn at age four. I began to do for myself what the medical experts predicted I could never do. As days, weeks, months, and years rolled on, so did my improvement. I look back on my early years and realize I am where I am today because of the "power of many" — as they all persevered and held the vision for me until I was able to hold it for myself.

Even today, I can feel the power of love that has encircled me throughout my life that is the collective vision held by many. Individually we have the healing power that was demonstrated on a grand scale by the likes of such ageless figures as Jesus, Mother Teresa, and Gandhi. This incredible power enables us to uplift one another. And like the Wright brothers who made flight in modern aircraft possible, so do those who care for and love us make flight possible for the human spirit as they hold the vision on our behalf until we can hold it for ourselves.

Holding the Vision for Ourselves

THE CONTINUING FLIGHT of the human spirit is only possible if individually we can hold the vision for ourselves, letting nothing hold us back. There will always be those who try to hold us down with their opinions and discouragement. This originates from their own sometimes narrow perception of our reality as well as theirs. If we allow the inner voice of the human spirit to speak loudly to us, we will then know, despite outside interference, when it is time to spread our wings. After personal preparation and acquiring the appropriate tools, each one of us must ultimately decide when to take our solo flight, when to blaze our own trails.

Blazing Grand Trails

ONE OF THE things that brings me the greatest joy is exploring the wonders of nature. There is nothing more exciting and, at the same time, calming to my soul as hiking and immersing myself in the great outdoors. As a teenager, on one of my visits to the South Rim of the Grand Canyon, I remember being at the "Bright Angel" trailhead and watching the hikers with their backpacks emerging from the bottom of the canyon. I vividly recall how I got on my pity-pot, feeling sorry for myself as I thought I would never be physically able to be one of those adventurous hikers. Ten years later, at the age of 31, my desire to hike to the bottom of the Grand Canyon intensified. With my newly-found confidence I decided that disability or not, I was going to hold to my own vision and hike to the bottom and back.

I set my goal to spend a year preparing myself before actually taking this grueling hike. During that year, it seemed like all I could do was eat, drink, and sleep hiking the Grand Canyon. I worked out at the gym daily — strengthening my legs and upper body. Weekends were taken up with hiking the local Red Rock Canyon — lengthening the distance each time I hiked to increase my endurance. Each day, I filled my mind with this dream that became my most important desire. The vision I held for myself became clearer and clearer as my focus was on what I wanted to achieve.

About five months before I was to take the hike, I went to see my doctor for a routine checkup. Unable to hold back the excitement, I told him I would soon be taking the eleven-mile trek down the Grand Canyon. I thought he would celebrate and encourage my effort, but instead, he looked at me with concern over what I had just disclosed. He proceeded to tell me if I took such a hike, I would quite possibly damage my legs and risk never being able to walk again.

I told him of the steps I had taken to prepare for this hike to somehow get his stamp of approval. But he refused to give me any approval or encouragement. Instead, he reiterated his stance that I should never consider such a thing.

I walked out of his office feeling intense discouragement! My vision was no longer real and I would only be able to see the hikers as they emerged from the canyon instead of being one. After all, my doctor, the one person I entrusted to counsel me over the concerns of my physical well-being had just advised me not to do something that was against all his medical advice. The choice was now mine.

I either had to take the doctor's advice and call off the hike or go with the knowledge and confidence that I could do anything I set my mind to. Never before had I ever felt such inner confidence — that I should proceed with every intention of making my dream my reality. Looking nowhere but forward, I didn't waste one step in continuing toward my dream, because I was confident that my preparations had been enough to fulfill my vision and make my dream come true!

At last, the highly anticipated day of my Grand Canyon hike arrived. I had all my gear, including a backpack loaded with the needed supplies, food, water, a sleeping bag, and first-aid kit to safely make the journey. But most importantly, I had my confidence! Family and friends who went along to support me again kept me encircled in their love and collective vision, holding onto my vision on my behalf.

With each step I took, I maintained a constant affirmative belief that what I was setting out to do was not only possible but realistic. I had to make a concentrated effort not to be invaded by negative thoughts, such as my doctor being right.

I made it to the bottom of the canyon, to Phantom Ranch, where I saw the flowing Colorado River. We set up camp for the night and as I went to sleep under the star-vaulted sky, I could hear the flow of the river that was not only calming but reinforced the fact I was in the process of fulfilling what had been a dream and distant reality only twelve months earlier. It was as if the river were telling me my truth — that most of my limitations were only self-imposed. If the river was capable of cutting and forming this beautiful wonder of the world, then I was also capable of expanding my possibilities!

The next day we took the rigorous upward switchback journey back to the canyon rim. As I emerged back at the trailhead, I could see the people looking down at us.

Another "Majestic Moment" overtook my entire being as I realized that I was now one of the adventurous hikers that, over ten years earlier, only wished I could hike the canyon. It was at that moment I realized the mighty power of personal vision and perseverance! It really works!

Once I got to the top of the canyon, I started sobbing like a baby. These emotions were not because of any physical or emotional pain, but from the personal realization that the very real majestic power of the human spirit can enable us to transcend our once perceived limitations — whatever they may be. As I looked out over the canyon's majestic landscape in gratitude for safely bringing me back, I knew that despite adversities, life's journey can be just as beautiful as the landscape before me, in all of its wonder and majesty. If we are patient enough with ourselves and each other, we allow the human spirit to take flight while blazing the grand trails of our lives.

When I returned home, I went to see my doctor again. I walked into his office with no changes in my mobility or physical condition. He immediately gave me praise for complying with his medical advice, as, in his mind, I looked as if I had not hiked the Grand Canyon. At first, I was apprehensive about telling him. I had returned from the hike just days prior. Then I went ahead and told him that I did in fact hike the canyon. He went silent for a moment with his head down. He looked up with tears in his eyes telling me I shouldn't have been able to exert my body like I had and return in such good physical condition. It was then he told me of his new-found conviction that the human spirit can and does at times defy even known medical logic.

Conclusion

BEING ABLE TO hold the vision, either for ourselves or someone else, with firm conviction, is more than perseverance or sweat on our brow. It is a call to enlarge that space within us that allows fear and self-doubt to be set aside to make room for the unfolding of our dreams and aspirations. It summons us to respond to ourselves and each other with unwavering faith and confidence that transcends time and space and knows no limitations. We can all agree this degree of faith brings with it a power that enables us to reach beyond the narrow perspective of ourselves, and each other, as we rise to new heights we never thought we could reach. It is more than a belief, an inner-knowing that can't be described, but felt. And although we should always give proper credit and heed to the experts, we should be able to realize that they may not always be aware of the mighty enabling power we possess — individually and collectively. This transcending power can only be emancipated if we inwardly hold the vision, act accordingly (outwardly) and allow the possibilities to unfold.

Too many people are thinking of security instead of opportunity. They seem more afraid of life than death.

—JAMES F. BYRNES

Chapter 5

The House of Cards

As a child, I remember watching my older sister and her friends create two teams to compete to see who could build the tallest house of cards. Of course, for obvious reasons, I was unable to participate. Observing seemed to be just as exciting. One could not help but feel the intense competitive pressure that filled the room as a card would be placed on top of cards until there was a tall tower that could collapse with the slightest breath. The slightest sneeze could be deadly. The team with the tallest house of cards left standing could claim victory, while the losing team, with disappointed looks on their faces, would be left to pick up a bunch of fallen cards, their efforts in vain and their sense of accomplishment shattered. Fortunately, it was just a game, and all would be forgotten in just a moment's time.

As we mature in years, we feel we don't have the time to play the childhood games we once played. We're too preoccupied with the things that grown-ups do like earning a living and getting things done to secure our lives in the real world. However, this doesn't mean we stop building our tower of cards that can tumble, leaving only scattered cards that symbolize our disappointments.

Our society has fallen victim to the epidemic of getting more material things to increase our sense of self-worth and disguise our insecurities. There is nothing detrimental in getting college degrees, good paying jobs and enjoying those things that we've earned through our efforts and hard work. Many of these things are necessary for maintaining not only ourselves, but our families. We should enjoy the fruits of our labor without feeling that somehow we're less spiritual or enlightened for so doing. But negative consequences surface when we define ourselves by our accomplishments and accumulations of things we believe are supposed to make us feel like we are worth something and that we matter. Self-worth lies within and does not fluctuate with external conditions or circumstances. If it does, then we need to take stock and see if it is genuine.

As our accomplishments and material possessions accumulate, they become like trophies on a shelf, where if "one or two are good" then "three or four are even better" — and so on and so on and so on. Keeping up with the Joneses becomes the grown-up version of building the house of cards. The truth is, when our foundations are built with our trophies instead of real inner strength, and change inevitably occurs, we are left with absolutely nothing on which to stand. We are left with nothing but unmet expectations and broken dreams. How unfortunate it is that many try to soften the blow, turning to the destructive use of drugs and alcohol, or even excessive work habits to get more trophies to quickly replace the ones they've lost.

Now I'm not pointing fingers at anyone except myself. I've had shelves of trophies and falling towers of cards that have ended up causing suffering and unmet expectations, and I expect I'll have more of these kinds of experiences as long as I'm alive. I think in writing this chapter, and all the other chapters of this book, I was first writing for my sole benefit — my process of self-discovery. But since we're all perfectly human, they just might be written for you as well. Doing our personal best to remove ourselves from the rubble of fallen cards and dusty trophies and continuing to learn and grow from what these sometimes uncomfortable experiences have to teach us in discovering our genuine wholeness creates our "Perfect Circles."

Growing from the Rubble

LIKE ALL OTHER valuable lessons put before us, when the weaknesses of our foundations are brought to the forefront, we have the opportunity to identify those aspects of ourselves that need to be fortified. Personal introspection allows us to see if our confidence and self-worth is conditioned on something outside of us instead of genuine inner-strength and confidence. We can't possibly realize that all of our experiences can be for our continued growth if we are overly preoccupied with life's disappointments — instead of the needed and expanded perspective we can gain from them. Yes, even when the cards tumble down, we are still able to grow from these often uncomfortable and undesirable experiences. Instead of perceiving the cards as debris or failures, we can look at them as just one more step in the realization of our full potential. Trees become distinct and separate from each other and the forest as a whole. A lost job offers the promise of a new and more fulfilling position because we have not only increased our practical knowledge base, but acquired new strengths and self-assurances that can take us down more fulfilling career paths. Old age brings increased wisdom and knowledge instead of loss of independence. No matter what life throws our way, we can transform what seems to be outdated rubble into growth opportunities. What we may have seen as a comfort zone becomes our uncomfortable zone that we must have the courage and confidence to move beyond.

Leaving Uncomfortable Zones

ONE OF MY social work positions was with Nevada's largest health maintenance organizations (HMO). I was employed there for seven years and made a substantial income with good healthcare benefits.

I had grown quite secure knowing I had a place in the productive world by making my own living and contributing to a society that puts emphasis on independence and pulling your own weight. My name badge, with my picture on it, was like a medal-of-honor that showed, I'm sure only to myself, an advancement in rank in the professional world and personal autonomy. Every day, though repetitious, provided me with a great amount of comfort in knowing that I had job security. In my mind, I had reached the highest pinnacle in my career, building a house of cards that could not fall — or so I would have liked to think.

My perceived comfort zone of a nice job with income to match became an uncomfortable zone, though at the time, I was too complacent to know it. Some of my coworkers left and were replaced by others who had preconceived ideas about my disability and how it might negatively impact my ability to do my job. Those new people questioned my work or took credit for it if they happened to approve of it. This prompted me to feel that all my efforts and expertise were not truly my own. My worth as a fellow professional dwindled, as did my worth as a fellow human being. The security I thought I had dwindled as I realized I was unable to control what others thought about me and my abilities. Each day brought more anxiety and uneasiness as my self-worth was on the chopping block.

Anxiety and many sleepless nights set in as I felt utterly helpless. Not only did the job no longer fulfill me, but I allowed it to put both my mental and physical health in jeopardy as well. Despite every indication that I should move on, I was unable to let go of the physical and emotional illusionary security. I held on for dear life and placed the job in such a high priority that working twelve hour days, weekends included, became routine. I believed that by working more, I could compensate for any inadequacies with which I allowed my coworkers to label me. I went so far as to frequently bring in donuts and Starbucks coffee to win over their approval. I gave away my weekends, my time to enjoy life. Providing incentives, bribing for approval didn't change the way my coworkers felt about me, nor did it eliminate the inadequacies I had allowed them to instill in me.

I learned a valuable lesson — that our inadequacies are not arbitrarily forced upon us by other people. We allow them to be placed upon us as we place the opinions others have of us, personally, professionally or both, so high on our already leaning house of cards that it becomes a determining factor of our self-worth. When our house of cards finally comes tumbling down, so does our self-worth — with nothing left to hold it up. The scattered debris of cards represents the sudden realization that the foundation we thought was holding us up is nothing more than an illusionary construct. We learn through these sometimes painful lessons that we are the only true builders of our unbreakable foundations. Sometimes we need to remove ourselves from certain opportunities, be it a job or whatever it is, as they can become the very rubble that impedes our forward motion.

My fears of losing my job were realized as the company laid off fifteen of its nineteen social workers. Each of us would need to re-apply for our positions due to our department's reorganization. Surely, I thought, the company would not be able to do without me, since I was proving worth with twelve hour work days! My interview came and went and the company I had given my life to for seven years decided that they could do without me.

The manager told me that I just wasn't what they were looking for. At first, I couldn't believe that those I had worked with and given my all for would turn on me and let me go! Questions like, "What did I do to make them not like me?" and "Could I have been better professionally so they couldn't live without me?" raced through my head at a million miles an hour. I searched to come up with a validating answer. And yes, I even thought that what had happened to me was extremely unjust because many of my coworkers that I had seniority over were allowed to remain in their positions.

At the time, I felt angered and betrayed. I felt like another casualty of discrimination from a mean and ruthless corporation that didn't care about its people. I thought about marching directly to an attorney's office to get even, fighting for my rights and get what I felt was rightfully mine as a disabled person. But wait! I was the one rallying around my own cause to be a fully functioning member of society, not wanting to be the helpless victim. Taking the litigious route would only put me in the driver's seat of being the victim again, a role I had worked so hard to vacate. Taking the legal route that some suggested was not only my right, but my obligation to stand up for the disadvantaged and downtrodden who could not speak for themselves would have turned me back into someone who was different and needed to be treated with kid gloves. This was certainly nothing I wanted for myself.

There were many before me who weren't physically disabled and were subjected to the same workplace slaughter I had just experienced. The firing also happened to the most physically fit and competent people in the company. It was utterly amazing to find books written to specifically address this unfortunate phenomenon, and nowhere in them did the writer state that it only happened to the physically disabled, or in this case, "John." My firing was a result of people's quest for power that came from widespread insecurities that we all sometimes try so hard to disguise. For whatever reason, they decided to let me go. I wasn't about to know all the reasons behind it, especially when it involved a multi-million dollar corporation where decisions are made every day, sometimes without rhyme or reason and that seem totally unfair.

Since I couldn't "have my cake and eat it too," being both victim and the one who simultaneously wanted to be treated like everyone else, the legal course of action was not my viable alternative and would certainly not, by any means, elevate my self-esteem. That particular job may have been taken from me, but the choice of how I would respond and who I wanted to become as a result was not taken away in the least.

My past experiences had given me enough of a solid foundation to leave the job I had been at for the past seven years with my head held high. I knew that this change would not alter the person I had become through this experience, as well as all other previous experiences. The growth and confidence I had acquired through what, at the time, seemed like a horror story, would be just a few more bricks with mortar toward building a more solid foundation. I had acquired heightened confidence — both professionally and personally. And although it would have been nice to feel needed enough to be retained by this corporation, there was a reassurance as I walked out of that office for the last time that the timing was right. The opportunity to stretch into new career paths was now put before me. The choice to either spiral up or down was yet again placed in front of me. I may have not been free that day to return to this particular job, but ultimately, I was still free to determine for myself what direction I could take.

The rich accumulation of my life experiences up until this point, made it possible for me to choose a more elevated perspective of the situation, and gladly surrender what was now just a name badge with a faded picture. I now was able to more fully comprehend that I was not losing a job and my identity, but gaining room for expanding my professional opportunities.

Hidden Treasures

OFTEN THOSE THINGS in our lives that can give us our greatest sense of illusionary self- esteem are the most fleeting and temporary. It is no wonder why some of the greatest philosophies and religions of the world teach us that true joy can only be found by looking within. In doing so, we discover that we are not our jobs, bank accounts, or even our physical appearances. We are an accumulation of the long-lasting residue left over from the experiences that are the successes, joys, pains, and of course, our disappointments. Even our perceived failures can be a tutoring moment in our long-term journey upward.

Instead of letting our failures bring us down, we can actually grow from them. The question is not if this can happen, but rather, do we have the patience and endurance to allow it to occur? It is only then, amid our life's falling house of cards, that the hidden treasures of wisdom can never fall or be taken away. These treasures, although sometimes difficult to discover, build character and like the growth rings of a giant sequoia, permanent markings are left on the soul that indicate growth.

Ageless Wisdom

ONE DAY, AS I counseled a client, I had the privilege of listening as she reflected on the process of aging. She was one of the greatest examples of how each season of life can bring an unfolding of who we want to become. She was an attractive woman who was dealing with a recent hip fracture that occurred when she fell while dancing on a cruise ship. She had lost her once cherished independence and self-reliance. The past was especially valuable as the years of youth had been such a vital part of her identity. She reflected on her dazzling career as a Las Vegas showgirl at the Stardust Hotel *Lido* Show in 1959, and the good times she once had that were now but a memory. She recalled "the good old days" when she was able to hang out in the chic casino lounges with people such as Dean Martin and Frank Sinatra.

Tears started rolling down her face as she told me about the dreaded days of old age. Days that were only once a distant thought were now a reality. Grief could be seen on her face, as if a dear friend had just been laid to rest. She feared that she would never go on another boat cruise again, much less dance. Some of her despair was recanted as she explained that all of her life experiences, up until the present, had made her into the person she was. She made it known that she really liked the person that she had now become.

It was then that her profound words of wisdom were offered as she stated, "Even though I hate getting old, I wouldn't go back one day. Getting younger might take away from what I've learned through the years. If younger means losing wisdom, then I want no part of it." In just our brief conversation, my client was able to shift her perception from seeing her advancing age as the cause of dwindling identity and emotional devastation to one of wisdom and satisfaction. Her well-earned maturity was the contributing factor in an increase in refinement and wisdom which strengthened the very identity that she feared losing just moments prior.

Realizing Our Worth

DURING MY YEARS of counseling individuals going through their own life transitions due to a major illness, I observed how we as human beings find our self-worth and identity through things that reside outside of ourselves and are, most often, of a temporary nature. If we are part of the human species, then we all have, at least sometimes on our life's journey, looked to things and people to bring about feelings of wholeness. In fact, a good portion of this book, if not all of it, deals with the quest to find this inner wholeness and to overcome the associated hurdles. I have come to believe that there is absolutely nothing wrong or harmful about seeking external validation and wholeness as long as it leads inward — where it ultimately needs to reside. Sometimes accepting that we have been taking an unnecessary detour facilitates our clearest recognition of the proper course that must be taken to solidify our foundation — so that we do not fall with the slightest shortness of breath. Our mistakes are not to be regretted but learned from.

What has been amazing to observe is how periods in our lives that are the most difficult and painful can, if we allow them, bring about the realizations that result in finding our genuine inner wholeness. These don't dissipate with life's transitory currents. Life transitions such as loss of independence, while discomforting, brings with it the pathways to discover that we're not what we do for a living, how much money we make, or even our ability to drive an automobile. While these things indeed can be counted as our life's accomplishments, we will, whether we like it or not, come to realize that they are truly not "us."

A License to Live

A PATIENT, I will call Harold, was referred to me for a counseling intervention as he was having extreme anxiety over his own life changes due to increased short-term memory loss. To look at Harold, you would think he was a very healthy, physically fit person for 77 years of age and indeed he was. He was still driving himself and his wife wherever they needed to go, as he had been doing for the last fifty years of their marriage. However, he was starting to make wrong turns on once familiar streets, and occasionally he would get lost and be unable to find his way back home. His faithful wife reported the unusual behavior to his doctor who ran tests, only to discover that he had the beginning stages of Alzheimer's. As it would be with anyone, the news was devastating. The doctor almost demanded that Harold surrender his driver's license so as to not put him, his wife, or anyone else's life in danger. I was called in by the doctor to ease the blow of the news.

The very first thing that came out of Harold's mouth was that if he could no longer drive, it would be like a death sentence. After inquiring why he felt this way, he immediately told me that his entire life had been centered on being able to drive. He continued, telling me that for a living he had always driven big trucks and that people depended on him. Even though Harold was fully retired and his wife was still able to drive short distances to meet their transportation needs, he felt worthless if he was unable to contribute as a reliable driver. His concern of not being able to drive far outweighed just being diagnosed with Alzheimer's.

After counseling with Harold on and off for three months, he reluctantly gave up his car keys and felt less of a person for having to do so. When I told him that I never had a driver's license and was never able to drive, having to creatively adapt to my own situation in order to meet my transportation needs, he stated that this was acceptable for me, but not for him. This brought a perplexing question to my mind. Why is it acceptable when others creatively adapt to their life changes, yet when it comes to our own lives, we go kicking and screaming?

Although the circumstances and degree of severity may be different, Harold's situation is no different. Whether we like to admit it or not, we've all had times when our self-worth was tied to something or someone else. We tend to allow ourselves to remain stuck in a changing world. Life changes, especially being newly diagnosed with Alzheimer's, are never pleasant for anyone, but when we attach ourselves to external things that must be present to give us self-worth and validation, we become unprepared to weather even a little storm. And like a tree, we must be deeply rooted and strong enough to stand tall and be flexible enough to bend so our branches don't break with the heavy winds of the seasons that always come with time and yes, age!

Although I don't know if Harold came to this particular self-realization, we don't require a driver's license to have a license to truly live. The only valid license we require is an expanded perspective to see that no matter what seems to be taken away from us, we have the capacity to rise above the occasion and grow from the experience.

The Power of Belief

OUR BELIEF IN ourselves, and ultimately the world around us, is the one thing that we can be sure will endure through life's storms and difficult transitions. It doesn't matter what we happen to label our beliefs, be it spirituality or inner-truth, if they expand our perspectives and buoy us up in time of need, then they are worth nurturing and hanging onto. It is belief that makes it possible for us to transcend the nature of those "things" that give us an illusionary sense of security and self-worth. Those "things" end up changing form or disappearing completely from our lives. I have to say that my personal spirituality has greatly assisted me in realizing that I possess more than just a physical body, but rather something that I have termed, "the human spirit." This human spirit seems more and more real to me and enables the body to move beyond life's adversity and barriers. With each encounter of adversity or challenge comes the realization that both the spiritual and physical dimensions of our existence can work together for both our long and short term benefit — to build both character and inner-strength. Without our physical experience, the human spirit would not know its own strength. The power of belief forms our personal map of the cosmos that can include or exclude our earthbound experiences. Such a map can remind us that what we do and experience has meaningful implications. My own physical challenges have forced me to see the spiritual and inner-dimensions of my life, compelling me to look beyond a world of limitations into one of endless possibilities. But by ignoring the very experiences that bring us personal growth and expansion, the metaphysics of self-denial creates frustration and ultimately victimhood.

The Metaphysics of Self-Denial

IN THIS QUEST I have, in times past, made desperate attempts to try and shun my physical reality, in high hopes of totally transcending to a higher or spiritual one — only to realize the disappointment and frustration of such an undertaking. Yes, I have discovered that transcending our perceived barriers to finding true joy and contentment in our lives does not come by denying that they do in fact exist, but rather, embracing them as a necessary part of realizing our inner and outer strengths.

During my early adult years, I started to dabble in what I would like to term the metaphysics of self-denial. I embraced the then popular New Age philosophy that all of our physical encounters are but self-created illusions. I was determined to become the most enlightened and spiritual person on earth by learning the technique of "Soul Travel" and have the ultimate out-of-body experience. I honestly thought at that time in my life that if I could just temporarily escape my imperfect body and enter some kind of cosmic reality where form and limitations did not exist, then I would finally reach the highest state of spiritual perfection. Of course, I wanted the luxury of returning to my illusion, my body, after taking this far-out journey. All I wanted was enlightenment, and come hell or high water, I was going to achieve it — even if it meant leaving my body.

I started this farout cosmic undertaking by going to the local New Age bookstore and desperately buying every book on the subject of Soul Travel I could find. Of course I also needed to accessorize with incense and chant music. Candles were out of the question — as I didn't want to burn down the house. Night after night I would set the mood and precisely follow the instructions on what one had to do to leave their body. I had the breathing and "*om*" mantra down perfectly. I would lie on my bed, sometimes for over an hour at a time, trying so hard to become enlightened — all without the desired result. I was never able to fly to the moon or the stars. There I was, still in my body. However, I did achieve the altered state of consciousness quite frequently called "sleep."

This desperate search for spirituality went on for about a year until I finally gave up with a drawer full of incense, chant music, and a bookshelf filled with every kind of "how to" book on successfully leaving the body. I will now admit that I was most unsuccessful! I was fortunate to have stopped attempting to have these out-of -body experiences before I went out of my mind. Instead of this venture leaving me feeling elevated, as was intended, it left me believing that I was a complete failure — not even good enough to have such an extraordinary experience.

Frustration set in as I honestly thought at this particular time in my unrelenting search for truth, as others were "flying around" and having the time of their lives, "poor little me" would have no other choice but to settle for a world with all of its troubles and strife. While I may have thought no enlightenment or inner-growth was coming my way, in reality, it was!

After much personal introspection, it finally hit me that genuine inner or spiritual growth does not come when we're off floating in some other dimension without form, but instead, it happens in the here and now within the boundaries of our physical bodies. We must learn to have joy and contentment in our own world before we can expect to have it in another. Our challenges here on planet Earth have more to teach us about the manifestation of the human spirit than any other experience we could ever have. This is neither to confirm nor deny the existence of unseen dimensions, as it is up to each of us to decide that which is or is not — based on our own personal beliefs and convictions. I bring this subject to the forefront to illustrate that no matter what our personal convictions are, be it religious or otherwise, acceptance of ourselves, where we are right now at this very moment, has universal relevance to each one of us in finding true joy and contentment.

We don't have to change form or be something different to reach a higher plane of awareness. All we have to be is a willing participant in the reality we are currently living, with all of its contrasts of suffering and joy. I firmly believe that without our challenges and adversities we would be unable to grow and have those moments when we can verify our own unique strengths and potential. The physical reality that we are each experiencing right now, even if we think we're a victim of unfortunate circumstance, is the one that has some nugget of hidden truth, tailored especially for us, to facilitate our inner or spiritual growth.

We don't have to like, enjoy, or be entertained by our experiences in order for them to, in the long or short term, make us stronger. While meditation and prayer are very real tools to increase our awareness and sense of the spiritual, we don't need to be in another galaxy or dimension in order for them to work. If we're not willing to seek our spirituality or inner truth by staying where we are at this very moment, with acceptance of what we really are in this life and meant to become, then we'll end up building another house of cards that will inevitably topple. When all is said and done, the metaphysics of self-denial does not work.

The Forces of Time

DEATH WILL INEVITABLY separate us from all that we now know and love — at least in the physical sense. To think about the moment when we experience this separation can bring a chill down our spine. The hard-hitting reality is that if we're the ones to die first, we will never again feel others' physical touch or embrace. Time becomes the phantom in the night, robbing us of the life we always knew, as it goes charging on, changing everything and in the end, taking from us the things we hold most dear.

After having lost someone close to them, some I have known vowed never to love again. If this is the reality we must all face at one time or another, then how do we continue to cultivate and nurture relationships without feeling that in the end there will be pain? How do we feel the joy of giving and receiving love if in the dark recesses of our minds we are only anticipating eventual loss? These are the pertinent questions of the soul. The answer can only come through loud and clear if we allow the human spirit to become dominant in our lives. It is only then that the phantom will transform itself into the gentle breeze that changes the landscape of what we have always known, while leaving the important part of our life's journey fully intact.

A Gentle Breeze

WHEN I WAS about twelve, I recall one bright sunny spring day when I was lying on a lounge chair in my grandparents' backyard. There was a gentle breeze blowing through the trees while my grandma was in the kitchen whistling, as she usually did. I distinctly felt totally secure knowing grandma was close by and my grandpa would be home shortly. We would soon be having dinner and I was sleeping over. What a feeling it was to know that those you love are close by. I remember feeling that I would never want anything to change from the way it was at that moment. The whole world felt like a safe place to be. But as I was lying there, basking in my security, something unusual happened to me — especially since I was only a twelve-year-old boy. My mind shifted to the thought that there might be a time when things wouldn't be the same, and grandma and grandpa wouldn't be there for me.

This particular instance stands out because it was the first time I contemplated mortality, not of myself, but of those I always wanted to remain close by. I don't even know why I would have thought about such a thing. My whole family was quite healthy and I had never attended a funeral.

I was so uncomfortable with the thought of losing those I loved that I remember going into the house and giving my grandma a big hug. I told her that I never wanted to be without either her or grandpa, or anyone else I loved for that matter. I distinctly recall her consoling and comforting response, "Sweet boy, we'll be together and love each other forever." Her response seemed so sincere that I put the thought to rest, as it seemed so far away. As I grew older, the Christmases and birthdays came and went with the grandparents and those I cared about always being there, as I had expected. These occasions became more priceless as those around me, including myself, got older.

In the following years, we would all go through many changes — not only in our looks, but in our circumstances. I had to come face-to-face with the fact that, as time moves on, people we love die! As each December 25th would come to a close, I would wonder if the next year would look the same. "Would the Christmas dinner table look as I wanted it to look, having everyone in their exact place or would there be an empty chair?"

That day came when my parents called me just a day after my birthday to tell me that my grandpa had died in his sleep from a heart attack. I immediately dropped the phone, thinking that it was finally happening; I was losing those I held dear. Four years later, my grandma made her departure from this life.

Both times, I was one of the pallbearers who carried the casket to the hearse. The moment was almost surreal as the hearse pulled away and I recalled my childhood experience lying on that lounge chair with the gentle breeze. My childhood fear was finally being realized. The Christmas dinner table indeed did look different. And guess what? There was absolutely nothing I could do about it, at least on a physical level.

Death can leave us feeling empty and above all, powerless. But when we go to the level of the soul, we find that the love we have for each other is as eternal as my grandma had once promised it would be. The memories we have can be as real today as when they actually happened if we will remember just the good parts. Death is transformed into the gentle breeze if it reminds us that we need to love and forgive others a little more often. There isn't time for regrets and grudges with one another.

At the time of this writing, I not only lost my grandparents but an older brother as well. I cannot stop time and the life processes we all have to go through. We must remember to show love each moment, then death becomes but a gentle breeze that blows through to remind us that part of our eternal soul, even time cannot change. A touch or embrace at the level of the soul can always be felt as it is that part of us that cannot die. Genuine love is the bricks and mortar that reinforce our foundation — ensuring that our spirit will never fall with the forces of time.

Conclusion

OUR HOUSE OF cards is built to topple when we seek to validate ourselves through the approval of others and things that are fleeting. It's when we surrender the need for approval and validation from others and things that are external to us that our life is transformed from a rather flimsy structure into the finest Ivy League University offering top-of-the-line educational opportunities. We are then truly free to explore life's expansive campus as we free ourselves from staying in one place, whether it is a job or any other situation which is not conducive to our continued growth and educational advancement. The question is not if we want to attend the University of Life, because, like it or not — we already are! But are we willing to take advantage of its many opportunities designed exclusively for learning how to reach our highest potential?

When our lives are built upon a firm foundation, we come to know that our challenges and even our accomplishments are not the substance of life, but if we allow it, fleeting scenes that make us stronger and more refined. Each card placed on our flimsy tower is transformed into solid block if we use all of our cumulative experiences, both the good and the bad, as tools to sculpt ourselves into what we are meant to truly become. When we do this, we see who we really are and have the potential of becoming. The pertinent questions should be not what we possessed or accumulated throughout the years, but how did we navigate ourselves through it all? Did we take advantage of every opportunity to advance ourselves inwardly — while being a full participant in the ebb and flow of life? More importantly, did we learn how to effectively differentiate the important from the unimportant stuff of life so when our house of cards did finally fall, we had a firm foundation on which to stand?

All we really need to accessorize ourselves in our journey is an expanded awareness that with each life encounter there is often times a well-disguised opportunity for building an inner-foundation that is permanent and secure. We don't have to shun the physical world to enter the spiritual, or vice versa, because both are ultimately one in the same — working together for our personal advancement.

Be not afraid of life. Believe that life is worth living,
and your belief will help create the fact.

—WILLIAM JAMES

Chapter 6

Seeing the Lights

IN 1983, MY family left Southern California to relocate in Las Vegas, Nevada. My father, who is a large-scale production show producer, was opening the impersonation show, *Legends in Concert*, at one of the major Strip resort hotels. Our family even got to live in the hotel, right smack in the middle of the excitement of the Las Vegas Strip to make it easier for my father to manage his new production. I remember my first encounter with the mammoth marquees and their dazzling neon lights, being utterly mesmerized. There wasn't a night that went by without noticing the lights. But after about six months, the light's dazzle disappeared, not that they actually went away or were turned off, but, as living in Las Vegas became routine, so did the lights, as they blended in with the day to night scenery of an ordinary desert town.

I found that in order to rekindle the dazzle I previously experienced, I had to consciously pay attention to the lights that existed all around me. Once I was willing to give my attention to the lights, the dazzle and excitement quickly returned. And so it is with the world that we see around us.

We have the choice to focus on whatever we desire. Yes, there's a lot of dimness or negativity in our world, but there are also a lot of lights or positive influences that exist. The most important question we can ask ourselves is on what are we to focus? And are we driving down life's "Strip" without even noticing all the magnificent lights around us?

The Epidemic of Seeing Only the Negative

BEFORE WE CAN see the light we must see the lights. This means that before we can see the good in our lives, we must learn to see the good that happens all around us. The terrorist attacks get front page news while random acts of kindness are lucky to make the last page of the "Living Section" within our local newspaper. Looking for the good around us does not mean we avoid or become numb to the tragedies that inevitably happen. Bad things do happen and to label them anything different is detrimental to our being able to identify the heroic and uplifting qualities that all of us innately have. Without our tragedies we wouldn't be able to see the resiliency and perseverance that brings to the surface the best part of humanity. This does not mean that we go around welcoming tragedies as a way of raising human consciousness. But we should always minimize adverse events, as much as possible, while looking for the good or the lights as a result of adjusting our lens for a clearer view.

The Lens Adjustment

ONE OF MY clients called me to help her find the lights in her world. Her voice sounded as if the tragic events of 9/11, the Asian tsunami, and Hurricane Katrina had hit her all at once. Her health was failing and she thought the entire world was, too. She expressed that life as she knew it was over; she might as well take an overdose of sleeping pills in the hopes of waking up in a better world. The loss of her husband two years prior only compounded her current news and emotional state. This day's grim news just added salt to her already grieving wound. She had developed an understood cynicism about the world and those she would leave behind. Her view was that she was left in her world — a world that was full of terrorists who blew up tall buildings and insane weather that killed innocent people. The good old days, as she called them, were but a memory. Although I wouldn't be able to bring back her husband or change the course of current events, I could perhaps facilitate the process in changing her view of reality.

During our time together, we discussed the possibility that perhaps the negative and emotionally painful recent events could bring to the forefront of our minds the good that people are capable of contributing to the world. Thousands of people rushed to these horrific scenes to volunteer their time and their lives to ease the pain and suffering of others. Even the glitz and glamour of Hollywood was put on hold as some of the biggest stars freely donated their time and talents to charities in order to help raise money just to try and get people's lives back to normal again. Families opened up their homes to help those who were uprooted by Hurricane Katrina to assist in the reestablishment of new lives. And 9/11 especially brought unity to the entire world as each one of us felt the common purpose in bringing about peace and unity.

After our many discussions, she didn't want bad things to happen in the world and her grief and loss was still on her mind — as can be reasonably expected. Now however, she was able to verbalize her expanded perspective that there was still a lot of good left in the world despite the pain. In the months ahead, she was able to express her newfound optimism in the lights that shine through the darkness that make life worth living.

Keeping the Focus

JUST WHEN WE think we've learned the skill of seeing the good around us, something steps in and the cynic within rears its ugly head.

The rose-colored glasses come off and go straight in the trash. The people around us turn from angels to devils, and the terror level alert goes from highly unlikely to extreme. When this sudden shift goes from an expansive perspective to a rather confining and limited one, we should recognize it and then accept it as a normal, but hopefully fleeting emotion. We shift our perspective when we become aware of the thoughts we don't want and gently let in the thoughts we do want. We can literally feel our bodies become relaxed from our tense state, as our perspective changes again.

Later, in my adult life, I have been persistent in always wanting to see the good in humanity. Hopefully, this outlook has improved my life as well as the lives of those around me. At times, I have found that this can be a rather difficult undertaking, especially when every day individuals living and working around us frequently seem to express negativity.

At times, I've thought that the most effective intervention would be to throw away the television set — so as to rid myself of the temptation to turn on CNN. Or better yet, move to an ashram in India, taking the strictest vow of silence so I wouldn't have the slightest chance of hearing a negative word from anyone. I did modify my intervention — to be more practical. Instead of getting rid of the television, I decided that watching more inspirational or educational programming would be a more balanced approach. In place of going to India, I decided to make an occasional retreat to my family's house in the beautiful mountain community of Lake Arrowhead, California. It is there that I get a sense of what utopia would be like, with its fresh air, tall pines, and shimmering lake.

The Return of the Mountain Utopia

ONE DAY, I was in the middle of the little quaint village area of Lake Arrowhead with my only pressing obligation to mail a letter that had to be postmarked that day. The post office looked like something from the classic Andy Griffith television show in Mayberry. What more could one ask for?

As I entered the one-room post office, I heard the bells that hung on the front door. They rang when the door was either opened or closed. Working behind a small desk was a grey-haired woman who could have passed for Mrs. Claus. I asked her if she could write the address on the front of the envelope that I had to mail after explaining to her that I needed assistance. I was unable to physically write because of my disability. She responded, "Sir, I have a million things to do today, and I won't help you. Who do you think I am anyway?"

Her response literally dumbfounded me; this was something I would expect to hear at the Midtown Manhattan Post Office at rush hour, not in this quaint little village. I was in utter disbelief, so I felt compelled to explain myself again as I was sure that she didn't understand what I was asking. So I did. She responded, "Sir, I completely understood you the first time, and the answer is no." Almost immediately I felt totally alienated from the beautiful mountain surroundings. I immediately thought that the years of getting to know this little community so well were but a memory. Little did I realize that at the same moment, an opportunity presented itself to have my mountain utopia return. Another woman, directly behind me in line, overheard my request for assistance. As I was about to leave the post office in anger, a woman, who was only a customer, tapped me on the shoulder and offered to help write the address on the envelope.

As I went outside, I have to admit that I was extremely angry, and above all disappointed, as my utopian dream bubble had just popped. The thought entered my head that if I weren't disabled, I would get more respect. My expectations of how people should treat others were simply not met.

Later that day, I told my brother what had transpired, and how the woman behind me in line had offered her help. I told him I couldn't believe that people could actually be this way. My younger brother, who wasn't about to sympathize, asked me one simple question that was so profound it immediately expanded my perspective of the situation. He simply asked, "Did you forget about the lady behind you who helped you?"

I suddenly realized that I had been so narrowly focused on the negative aspects of this experience that I totally ignored the positive. The reality of the situation was, for whatever reason, this particular post office worker was not about to help me. Maybe she was just having a bad hair day or the customer she helped earlier that day gave her a run for her money. Most likely her response had absolutely nothing to do with me being disabled.

But in that same situation was a person who was willing to help! I just needed to see the good that was already there.

Seeing the Good in Others

ONE OF THE greatest blessings that can come from any kind of adversity is seeing the good in people as they render random acts of kindness. We may hear stories of people demeaning others with differences and think that humanity is intolerant and cruel. In my own experience of living in this body, I have discovered there are those who spread intolerance and cruelty, but there are far more who are willing to extend their hand, whenever possible, to make someone else's day a little easier. Whether opening a door for someone or flashing a friendly smile, these little acts are the lights surrounding us every day and they should never take second fiddle to the negative things that we allow to infiltrate our lives. When times get rough, sometimes seeing the good in others can be just the antidote we've been looking for.

Laugh! It's the Samsonite Sled Ride

I WANTED TO fit in so much when I started my undergraduate studies as a freshman. My dream was to be just another student. To do this, I took the first big step and bought a new Samsonite briefcase to be able to carry my notebooks, books, and any other supplies — without dropping them and be noticed as someone who might have special needs. I was making my way to Business Law 101 class that happened to be held on the second floor of the huge business complex. My briefcase was in hand and I felt that I was really fitting into the college scene — almost ready to conquer anything. The campus was wall-to-wall students — all trying to get to class. As I almost reached the top of the stairs, I fell forward. The scene turned to slow motion as I realized the worst was happening. My dream of fitting in was just that, a dream, and I had just awakened!

Luckily, I landed on top of my Samsonite briefcase and slid to the bottom of the stairs without a scratch. Although I was not physically injured, I was emotionally devastated. There I was on the ground, feeling humiliated that I had fallen down and knowing that everybody ever created in the known universe, or at least in my mind, was looking at me.

I looked up and out of the corner of my eye I saw a girl standing there, looking down and laughing. She said, "If you could have only seen yourself coming down those stairs on that briefcase. That must have been some kind of ride." She reached out her hand to help me back to my feet, making sure I was dusted off and put back together to go on my way. This little bit of encouragement made it possible for me to get back up and move on — knowing there was at least one kind heart when I needed it most.

Figuratively or literally, we all fall down along our journey through the labyrinth called life. Each of us, like the girl who offered me her assistance, is capable of picking up others and empowering them to move forward, assuring them that they matter. That girl not only helped me up physically, but emotionally as well. Though she looked down and laughed, I realized she wasn't laughing at me, but at the situation of sliding down a flight of stairs on a Samsonite briefcase — because it was funny. She helped me to lighten up on life and learn to not take myself so seriously. At that moment I began to realize that being overly serious about ourselves can weigh us down, making every life experience one of apprehension and uncertainty.

Expectations and Reality

WHEN WE EXPECT the best from ourselves and others, we have the best odds for success. Our expectations create a field of either positive or negative energy around us and within each other. We've all had times when we get out of bed in the morning and expect the day ahead to be bad — and guess what, it is! I can't explain the mechanics of this phenomenon, nor is it the purpose of this book to do so, other than to personally testify that it does occur.

The Day from Hades

ONE DAY, FOR no particular reason, I woke up feeling incapable of doing anything right. I felt like a total loser. At first, I wasn't sure if I should even get out of bed. I was sure as the sun came up that I was going to have a bad day. I knew I would be able to do nothing right. I proceeded to get dressed and try to change my attitude. I even tried reading a few positive affirmations I had pinned up on my bulletin board like, "It is a great day," but nothing worked to change my expectations of the day ahead.

Being that I am unable to drive a car, I have learned to use public transportation quite well. On this particular day, I boarded the bus to work, as I usually did, and was greeted by a new driver. As I attempted to put my money in the change slot, I was shaking more than normal and was having an extremely difficult time. I ended up dropping my loose change all over the place. To my surprise, the driver ordered me off the bus, as he thought I was too intoxicated or on an illegal substance. I couldn't believe what was happening, but he was treating me exactly how I was currently feeling about myself. I had turned into a sloppy drunk reject, even though I was properly dressed and on my way to work with a drug and alcohol blood level of zero. I told the driver that I was not drunk, but on my way to work at one of Nevada's largest HMOs. I think this bit of information may have incriminated me even more. He threatened to call the police if I didn't immediately exit the bus, which I willingly did, being there was a ten thousand dollar fine and a mandatory jail sentence of six months for anyone refusing to obey a bus driver. For me, this was the day from Hades.

While I can neither confirm nor deny any direct correlation between this humiliating incident and the way I was feeling about myself that day, I do believe it can give us all some food for thought. Do the beliefs and expectations we hold about ourselves influence how others respond or react to us? In some way, I believe they do!

I don't believe there's anything mystical or mysterious about this phenomenon, but rather, our internal voice about ourselves that determines how we respond to others. How we hold ourselves, walk, and talk on the outside is inevitably affected by what's going on in the inside. Even if we're dressed for success, without expecting it, we cannot achieve it. I decided after this incident that before leaving the house, it is imperative that my thoughts are always in sync with how I want the rest of the day to respond to me. I'm not saying we create our own reality, like a magician pulling a rabbit out of a hat, but by observing our reality more closely, it does make one wonder.

Leaving Room for Growth

JUST AS OUR expectations may determine how we personally respond to the outside world, and vice versa, so the expectations we have of others may determine how they will respond to us. I have seen this phenomenon manifest itself countless times while working in my capacity as a social worker.

I have worked alongside many medical professionals, all with differing opinions and viewpoints of the same patients. Sometimes we would meet as a disciplinary team in order to reach common goals to improve a particular patient's quality of life. Amazingly, it would often seem that we were each discussing a totally different person. We could never seem to come to a consensus that would enable us to help or heal the patient, as we all had different expectations and beliefs about who we were trying to help. Our meetings usually accomplished little as patients were pigeon-holed into individual boxes — each with a lid and label. No one was willing to listen to what the others had to say. Only the "textbook" cases were used as models to determine one's ability to overcome adversity — instead of the resiliency of the human spirit, which has proven itself countless times, in transcending known clinical barriers. Even within the medical profession, the expectations physicians, nurses, and social workers have of their patients can be as detrimental or as healing as a newly-sharpened scalpel.

Taking the Lid Off

THERE HAVE BEEN times that a physician or a nurse has come to me and requested that I see their "problem patient" — as they are commonly referred to. These particular patients, and even their caregivers, are often described as "unruly," "uncooperative," a "train wreck." Even HMO executives, who sit in their corporate ivory towers, refer to the very people they are supposed to provide care for as their "cost liabilities."

People become statistics in a cost-analysis report instead of a person who has feelings and expects to live life to its fullest. Every time these negative labels are placed on someone, so are expectations of how they will perform — leaving no room for movement in a positive direction. Other descriptive details also included how patients were "hopeless cases" and needed to go straight to nursing homes as their families or caregivers were not capable of caring for them. Even having a master's degree did not exempt me from being labeled, "the mentally retarded social worker," by the same people who were providing care for the big HMO. I, too, have been evaluated by these same professionals and I felt labeled and sometimes still do by their faulty preconceived judgments and expectations that don't reflect my abilities.

I feel that it is my professional obligation to view these patients and their families with the highest of expectations that they have the inner ability to make the best choices for themselves. It has been my challenge to see people's inner power to problem-solve and inwardly heal themselves. By wanting to see the best in every situation, I would often see something quite different than what was originally reported to me by a nurse or physician. It was in these particular encounters that I saw patients and their caregivers go from "unruly" to scared and uncertain about the future and from "uncooperative" to having extreme difficulty adjusting to losing independence and control of their lives. I found that in most of the particularly undesirable behavior cases, "acting out" was a call for help — normal human fear and insecurity resulting from difficult life transitions and the anxiety that commonly accompanied them. This power of expectation applies not only to healthcare profession-als, but to all who want to be in the profession of the living. It takes courage to approach another without preconceived ideas and beliefs. We cannot put sanitary labels and limited expectations on them in order to avoid the sometimes uncomfortable task in developing a genuine understanding.

It's often easier to label those who are different than it is to make a genuine connection. We sometimes neglect taking a second look at someone else's disability, religion, culture, and social status, among other types of diversities. Truly living means we tap into our healing capabilities as we broaden our expectations of others, as well as ourselves — leaving the lid off, enabling the possibilities to escape the small box we may have put them in. We need to remember that our "Perfect Circle" is perfect only because we shape it with our uniqueness and not our sameness.

Collectively, we must take the road less traveled by admitting with all the humility we can muster that we don't know another's potential, but we have the courage to learn. Instead of seeing the street beggar as someone who is always taking from society, he could be seen as someone who could give something back if given the proper training and opportunity. Just as we cannot see the sun without pulling up the blinds, we cannot see the divine or best in each other if we don't take the lid off our expectations.

Conclusion

WE CAN CHANGE our reality, but not in the way we might think. We don't have the luxury of a magic wand or a genie in a lamp. This is not to say that what one usually considers to be a miracle can't happen. But for the most part, our ordinary everyday miracles happen when we decide to shift our focus. The opportunity to make the shift presents itself when we are confronted by circumstances that throw us off-balance and narrow our point of view.

The barriers to remain in balance don't simply disappear just because we want them to. The effort to expand our view is ours — seeing the good, even when it is difficult to find. The little quaint mountain utopia I longed for didn't change — only my perspective as I was able to shift to see the good that had been right before me all along.

Instead of all the people who looked and laughed at me on that crowded university campus as I slid down those stairs, somebody was there to assure me that I was perfectly human, as she reached out her hand to help me back to my feet. If we want to see the lights around us, we must first recognize they are there to brighten our life experience.

It's good to be alive!

—JACK RUSHTON

Chapter 7

The Light Habit

ADAPTING OUR VISION to see the lights, or good in our lives, is not possible unless we first learn what I would like to call the "Light Habit." Just as plants attract light through the process of photosynthesis, we also attract the lights or good into our lives by getting into the habit of being in a state of thankfulness. As talked about in the previous chapter, attracting good things into our lives is, for the most part, acknowledging that which is already there, if we adjust our focus. This may not always be easy, especially if we are going through a depressed period where there's nothing to be thankful for, or so it may appear. But, as with forming any habit, we have to start making a conscious effort to think of something we're thankful for — even if there seems to be nothing in sight. If this is the case, then we can be thankful for a bright, sunny or even rainy day. Or, if we need the stretch, be thankful for that last bit of toothpaste in the tube after rolling it to the very end. No matter where we direct it, having thankfulness etched in our hearts opens the portal to the soul to receive the good that is right in front of us.

Having Appreciation for Life

IN WORKING WITH a hospice, I have been blessed to have the opportunity to experience the genuine gratitude in those who are terminally ill. Many people who have been told they have only a short time left to live discover a deeper appreciation for life. It's not unusual for them to express how unfortunate it is to have to be given a death sentence in order to see life from the perspective of gratitude. I have heard terminally diagnosed patients say they had never experienced the intense wonder of a sunset or a blossoming flower until they were told these beautiful life experiences were about to be taken from them. For many, the grim prospect of pending death can transform the recipient into the greatest teacher in how to truly live life to its fullest.

The people who appear on our life's path can be our greatest teachers. They teach us how to embrace the true art of living and they all add a little more joy and thankfulness to our lives, despite the bumps in the road. Our fellow life travelers who appear to be living with an unfortunate set of circumstances are the people who teach us the most about strength and the transcending quality of the human spirit that we all possess. They are our teachers who show us that angels actually do exist in the here and now in the form of all of "us" who reach out with compassion to make another's journey a little easier. They give testimony that life itself is truly a giant institution of higher-learning, customized especially for us. And our attendance and attention is vitally important!

Tom's Angels

I HAD THE opportunity of getting to know one such individual by the name of Tom. Looking at Tom, purely from a physical level, you would have to conclude that he was one of the unluckiest people alive. He lived with uncontrollable insulin-dependent diabetes. At our first meeting, he had end-stage renal disease — his kidneys no longer functioned. To stay alive, he needed to be connected to a dialysis machine that acted as his artificial kidney. He received dialysis three days a week for three hours each day at a local center, where about thirty other people receive this same life-sustaining treatment. Tom had also been diagnosed with both brain and lung cancer and received radiation treatment five days a week in order to shrink the tumors. As one could only imagine, he was exhausted and did not feel well the majority of the time and he made frequent trips to the emergency room. But if you ask Tom about his life, he'd always respond that he certainly should be counted as one of the lucky ones. Not lucky because of his physical health but lucky because of his resilient human spirit that could not be threatened by any physical illness — unless he allowed it. The extraordinary thing about Tom is that he never allowed it!

At first, one would surely think Tom was off his rocker for sounding so optimistic when physically there was so much wrong in his life. But after talking to Tom and getting to know him for the individual he was, you and I could quickly come to know that he really meant it; that he inwardly counted himself as one of the luckiest people alive.

Although Tom assured everyone that he would rather not have to deal with his physical adversities, in the very next sentence, he assured us it was those very adversities that taught him to see all of life through the eyes of gratitude. He had many days of suffering from poor physical health; however, those days when he felt just a little less pain, he celebrated with much gratitude. He allowed his attendance in the school of hard knocks to build him up, rather than tear him down. One of the ways he learned the skillful act of overcoming his challenges and adversities was by giving simple notice and thanks for those things and people in his life that added both beauty and comfort to it.

One small but profound demonstration of this attitude of gratitude happened when we were sitting together in his doctor's office. He brought to my attention a framed matted red rosebud hanging on the wall. His intention of pointing out the rose was not to promote needless casual conversation, but to comment on how beautiful and perfect it was. For most people in the room that day, this flower may have been nothing more than a simple wall decoration to glance at while getting more impatient as they waited for the doctor to enter the room. But for Tom, it was a wonder of creation that not only deserved notice, but a true acknowledgement of the things that made up his beautiful world. Even more amazing on this particular day, Tom had extreme difficulty breathing, making him extremely sick, almost to the point of needing to call 911. But despite his lowly outward physical condition, inwardly, his spirit was as healthy as a marathon runner who had just won the race. Very much alive, he was still able to take time to smell the flowers, and above all, give thanks.

When I saw Tom the next day, he was feeling much better. The first thing he told me was how good he felt compared to the day before. He was thankful for being able to get more air to his lungs and breathe more freely. Just to be able to hear Tom give such gratitude for a body function that most people take for granted gave me another "Majestic Moment" where all of my mundane immediate concerns and worries were put into their proper perspective.

Those who have had the opportunity to know Tom will undoubtedly say that they have become a better person. When world events seem to cloud our humanity with negativity, with all of the violence, hatred and unrelenting quest for power, Tom had the ability to bring one gently back to true reality — that we really do live in a loving universe with literal guardian angels all around us. He didn't claim to have supernatural abilities or access to unseen dimensions where angelic beings have been known to live. What he did have was the ability to count those that love and care for him as living proof that guardian angels really do exist in the here and now.

Prior to getting ill, Tom worked as a driver for a small towing company owned by a married couple, John and Terese. While he was able, Tom helped to take care of Terese as she was recovering from cancer. But as his health started to decline, the roles were reversed, and the Smith family started caring for Tom. He had no immediate family in the area, so they later took him into their home when he became too ill to care for himself.

John opened up his home for someone who was once only one of his employees. He also sought to willingly care for another, even after caring for his wife as she battled her own health issues. This relationship is a manifestation of how true compassion is the absolute best of what human beings can offer one another in the time of need.

As Tom was leaving his doctor's office, the nurse commented to him on how many people he must have that love and cared for him. He responded in a simple but profound way by saying, "There are guardian angels all around me." After hearing this, I realized that this was indeed a reality for him. People like Terese, John, even the doctors and nurses, along with many others who have helped Tom are sure to be counted among his repertoire of genuine guardian angels. As he continued to travel his bumpy road of adversity, he was comforted knowing he would never have to endure it alone.

One might think that all of his prayers consisted of pleadings to absolve him of his personal adversity. To the contrary; his petitions to his higher power included the blessing of the lives of those around him as well as expressing gratitude. I was moved to tears as Tom told me that he had been inspired once to pray with his doctor while he was receiving a dialysis treatment. At first I thought it unusual for a doctor to pray with one of his patients. After all, by this time in my career, I had been around quite a few doctors myself and had never heard or seen such a thing. But after Tom described his doctor and the compassion he had for each of his patients, my hope was renewed that the medical profession still had some real healers left in it.

To me, that act of a patient and his doctor praying together seemed to become an essential and natural part of any effective medical treatment. And even though a curtain partition was drawn around them for privacy, the prayer offered by Tom blessed not only those who attended dialysis alongside him, but all those who provided for his medical care. He asked that the entire dialysis center be under the same heavenly protection as if it were a holy sanctuary. It became very clear, after hearing of Tom's heavenly petitions, that in order to see guardian angels, you first need to be one.

His physical life ended during the writing of this book and he will be missed by all. His eulogy was nothing less than a celebration of the human spirit's ability to make positive change a reality within all who beckon to its gentle call.

The "Perfect" Eulogy

As I was in the process of completing the final chapter of this book, Tom passed away. After attending his funeral, I realized that I was not yet complete in my writing. I felt moved to return to his story and perhaps tell the greatest part — the part that confirms our ability for positive change. After having heard friends and family eulogize him at his funeral, I realized that although I had the opportunity to develop a close relationship with Tom in the course of over a year, I did not get to observe the power of human transformation that he so masterfully demonstrated to those who knew him longer.

I did not know the full Tom, the one who took a stand to change his life, and actually did it. Memories of him were fascinating as his friends told of a man who only five years earlier had been down in his own pit of alcohol and drug abuse. Words like "crass and vile" were used to describe him during this turbulent period of his life. This person I never knew was also credited with being so self-absorbed that he cared little, if at all, about whom he happened to hurt or offend.

As John, Tom's close friend and caregiver, along with other friends and family spoke their most cherished thoughts of him, they spoke of an individual who decided to turn toward the possibility of reaching out for a better life — and never once looked back. Once his decision was made to better himself, he gave himself no other alternative but to do so. I'm certain that his example will be a beacon of hope that it is not beyond our capability to make constructive changes in our life's journey. We are always a work-in-progress — innately striving to meet our full potential. We are never powerless to choose what direction we will go and it's people like Tom who come into our lives to teach us something a little more about successfully completing our own "Perfect Circles."

Days before his passing, Tom told me he felt prepared to die — as he had set his life straight. I realized, while writing this book, that his life demonstrated something of importance for us all. Tom had the "perfect" eulogy because like "Perfect Circles," it told of another individual, himself, who through his life's experiences came to a point where he realized, if only for himself, his true potential. No, he wasn't always the person people pictured during the last five years of his life. But in spite of his rough years being the "crass and vile" person he once had been, he ultimately became the person he wanted to be and others could see as an example of how life can be used as a process to triumph over human weakness. We are never hopeless causes, but rather, diamonds in the rough just waiting to be refined and polished. Because we can't really know one's whole story without reading it from cover to cover, I don't feel I could honestly have completed a book on *Perfect Circles* without having shared Tom's "perfect" eulogy.

Being Grateful for People in our Lives

THERE'S NOT ONE of us, if we took an insightful look at the landscape of our lives, who would not have cause to be grateful for the people in them. As previously discussed, the real angels are the people who give us a boost, while ultimately we are the only ones who can completely lift ourselves. Whether it's a parent, grandparent, sibling or friend, these are the people who have, at pivotal times, facilitated the human spirit in us in our flight toward wholeness. When adversity and hardship pushes us to its seemingly narrow corner, we have the opportunity to find our way out by realizing that the love we unconditionally receive is the power that can indeed assist us in realizing that we really can fly. Having another person totally present with us, if only for a brief moment in time of need, is one of the sweetest gifts. What more do we need to be grateful?

How Sweet It Is

AT AGE FOUR, I was still unable to walk unattended. My grandmother took it upon herself to teach me how to walk by appealing to my extreme affinity for M&M-without-peanut candies. Like in the 1982 movie, *ET*, she would trail these treats around her house as an incentive to get me to walk on my own. The further I would walk, the more M&M candies I would be able to collect — all for myself.

Day after day she would diligently get me to improve my walking ability. Her diligence and love had a big part in making me into the person I am today. Looking back on this experience, my grandma taught me something vitally important about those who truly love us. Later in my life, she told me that as hard as it was for her, she would allow me to take a fall or two while she was teaching me to walk. Of course, before allowing me to take my occasional plunges, she would always make certain that I was in a secure place where I would not have the slightest chance of getting severely injured.

She went on to explain that while she had to resist the temptation to make sure I would never fall, by immediately intervening, she knew in her heart-of-hearts that the only way I could effectively learn anything would be by trial and error. There would be a few falls here and there while trying to get those M&Ms, but through it all — I learned to walk on my own! How can we ever learn to do anything effective in life unless we have the opportunity to make a few mistakes along the way?

Sometimes we demonstrate genuine love and compassion when we allow others to learn their own lessons through trial and error. To always intervene and prevent another from falling down, or make errors, no matter what or who they may be, impedes one of life's greatest lessons — to learn and grow. I now realize some of the most recognizable periods of learning and growth came from the ability to take a few plunges, either figuratively or literally, while others stood by with their love and support. Sometimes we miss the sweet opportunities to be thankful for the people in our lives who have prevented us from experiencing the difficult learning curves, when we only credit them for helping us. In retrospect, I now am able to recall those times when I thought people, be it my parents, school teachers, or friends were sitting idly by watching me struggle, they were actually showing me their greatest expression of love and compassion.

Every time I open a bag of plain M&M candies and slip one into my mouth, the emotion of gratitude washes over me as I revert back to that time when my grandmother's only wish for me was to take a few more steps toward a more independent and fulfilling life. I remember how sweet this life can be when we have people in it to love and care for us as they just want us to take one more step toward wholeness.

Many of us may not have loving and caring people readily available to them in their own lives, and for this, I realize I have indeed been fortunate. However, this does not mean that the rest of us are without the opportunity to have caring and loving relationships come into our lives. It only means that we have an opportunity to be more loving and caring ourselves. Not one of us, no matter what our circumstances, is left without a sweet bag of candies to open if we will extend ourselves to the oftentimes well-disguised opportunity of showing our gratitude.

Being Grateful for What We Have

SOMETIMES WE MIGHT have cause to believe that Lady Liberty has lost her sex appeal and the United States is not the greatest country in the world in which to live.

Traveling across the globe as far as Russia can give us cause to return home, only to say we are grateful for those things that we once took for granted.

From Russia with Gratitude

MIKHAIL GORBACHEV, THEN chairman of the fading Communist Party, had torn down the Iron Curtain in 1991, making this once secretive part of the globe open to Western influence. It was in that same year that my father's Las Vegas show, *Legends in Concert*, toured the former Soviet Union. My family was privileged to see this part of the world and experience its wonderful people. The amazing thing about what we observed during our three week visit was just how impoverished this country was. Its reputation for being a world superpower, second only to the United States, quickly diminished as hundreds of their hungry citizens waited in lines that were hours long just to purchase a loaf of bread. Large food markets, that we too often take for granted, were non-existent. The food served in our hotel dining room was marginal at best. However, not one of us on the tour had the audacity to complain. After all, we had food in front of us, in plentiful amounts, as compared to the rest of the country's citizenry.

When we returned to the states and resumed our normal lives, we could not help but give thanks for the things we once took for granted. Being able to go to the supermarket and purchase an immense variety of food, and not stand in long lines, was an experience that could have brought us to our knees in humility and overwhelming gratitude.

I had a newly discovered sense of gratitude for being able to live in a country that was able to provide such opportunities and abundance to its citizens. Now when I happen to be filled with cynicism about national politics and the corruption that sometimes infiltrates with its occasional scandals and cover-ups, I immediately bring myself back into reality, and remember that despite its shortcomings, I still live under a political umbrella that provides for my every need. Just the ordinary supermarket loaded with every type of food item we need and don't need should give us more than enough justification to be grateful.

Yes! I still have days when I lose this perspective, wishing that some of our leaders could be more trustworthy and the country in which I live could be a utopia. But as with everything, we can again widen our perspective by acknowledging that nothing in life will ever be just as we want it to be. At the same time, we need look no further than right in front of us for those things that we can be truly grateful for every day.

Conclusion

WHILE THE END-OF-LIFE and adverse situations can definitely bring us a deeper appreciation for life, we don't necessarily need them to start breaking into the Light or thankfulness habit. Each day presents new opportunities to be thankful for something or someone. As we take full advantage of these opportunities, we will inevitably shift our focus to the lights that we attract or that which is good in our lives — no matter how bumpy the journey may seem.

When we practice being in a state of thankfulness, our whole body feels lighter. Like a plant, we grow toward the light for only one reason — because we can see it! It's no wonder that this is the "Light Habit!"

To be yourself in a world which does its best to make you someone else means fighting the hardest battle that any human being can fight, and never stop fighting.

—e. e. cummings

Chapter 8

Becoming Perfectly Imperfect

DURING ONE OF our family retreats to Lake Arrowhead, I had an insightful conversation with my aunt Leslie. She told me about a time when her then six-year-old son Justin drew a picture of a surfboard with his name in the middle of it on her antique school desk — with a black permanent felt tip marker. At first, she couldn't believe her little boy had damaged the unique piece of furniture, and started to scold him. As she looked at his innocent face, she could not bring herself to do so, but instead, she realized that he was only doing what all healthy children do, creatively expressing who they are. She started to get rid of the childhood drawings by sanding its now flawed surface. As she started the process of bringing the desk back to its original condition, she suddenly realized that it was now "perfectly imperfect." Although the permanent marker drawing would have ruined the polished look for most, for my aunt Leslie, the same drawings made it a genuine original. The once-perceived flawed surface was now perfect in her eyes, as it had been given its one-of-a-kind look by the hand of her now-renowned young artist, her son. She displays the desk in her home with the surfboard and her son's name clearly visible for all to see, because, for her, she would not have the little school desk look any other way.

As I've had the chance to reflect on this rather simple story about the love between a mother and her child, I realize it may also have a rather profound message for all. The antique school desk represents each of us as a clean slate; the child's creative hand represents all of life's experiences that through the years are drawn upon us. The minute we first enter the world, experiences make their marks on us. Unique marks, lines, and grooves are drawn upon us that make us true originals. Some of the markings may be undesirable to look at, but in retrospect, we find that we would not be without them because of the personal growth they have provided. Our personal desks or life stories cannot be duplicated as they are our own. They are uniquely ours and especially tailored for our benefit. No matter how flawed or damaged we think we are, it is time to put away the sandpaper and look beyond the initial appearance of imperfections so that the perfections can be allowed to clearly come into view. When all is said and done, and we have made our final exit from this life, our only desire should be to be able to look back on our own personalized school desks with the sure knowledge that it was not the polished finished wood that made it perfect. It was the marred wood with its permanent felt tip markings drawn by the hands of our life experiences that made us "perfectly imperfect."

It is unfortunate that there are many of us who never fully realize what we have to offer. Like the marred school desk, we simply want to sand away the imperfections or throw in the towel, giving up because we simply cannot grasp our sometimes well-hidden attributes and perfections. The amazing thing about uncovering our individual and collective perfections is that acceptance is all that is required. We don't need to rid ourselves of disabilities or those things we cannot change about ourselves. If we or another walks, talks, or looks different, we don't need a magical potion to make those innate differences disappear — because there's absolutely nothing wrong with having them in the first place! All we need to do is have the willingness to creatively adapt to them, focusing on our abilities, allowing ourselves to be our personal best.

Most of us have the healthy desire to want to improve ourselves and we want others that we love to do the same. This doesn't mean that we improve by wanting to become something we're not, comparing ourselves to some ideal we've imposed upon our minds of the "perfect" person. The term "perfect" can alienate and divide us both internally and externally if we use it exclusively to describe our imagined ideal person or circumstance.

As already mentioned in Chapter 1, our perception or definition of "perfect" needs to be broadened to take into account our individual differences and abilities. What a dysfunctional world it would be if the only people considered perfect were doctors. If everyone strived to meet this expectation, then we would only have doctors to serve us. This would do little good if we needed a contractor to build a house.

While being a doctor is a noble and worthwhile profession, in order to successfully function, our world needs people to be willing to serve in a variety of professions, each contributing and worthwhile. As the familiar saying goes, "When they made us, they threw away the mold," and thank goodness — or we'd all be in a mess.

Elevating Our Perspective

I'VE STRIVED TO elevate my self-talk and see the good that is already in my life. When people ask me how I'm doing, I've become accustomed to saying, "perfect!" After all, if those I care about and I are in good health and the "sun's still shining," why would I want to respond any other way? But I sometimes forget that not everyone has broadened the definition of this term to encompass our differences, abilities, and disabilities. There have been times that I used this term, "perfect," to describe how I was doing — leaving others quite dismayed. They couldn't comprehend how anyone could possibly meet this ideal, especially since the natural human condition will always tag us with our personal flaws. What they didn't know was that I was using the term "perfect" in its relative "human" sense — to fit my unique abilities and even disabilities.

The "Perfectly" Imperfect Response

ONE OF MY coworkers once asked me how I was doing. I responded by saying, "perfect!" She then asked me how I could be perfect because of my obvious physical disability. My first reaction was amazement — how anybody in her right mind could have the audacity to ask such a ridiculous question. I quickly realized that she was defining this term from an absolute perspective based on her prior knowledge of its meaning. Without engaging her in a philosophical conversation or reacting in a derogatory way, I responded "Well I guess I'm perfectly imperfect." She then made a remarkable human connection by ending our brief conversation with, "Well, I guess we're both in the same boat because I'm imperfect, too." Reflecting on her last statement reminded me that genuine acceptance of who we are as a species requires that we feel comfortable with labeling ourselves as imperfect.

It's no wonder that an authentic Persian rug always has at least one flaw sewn into it to signify that amidst the beautiful symmetry of life there are always imperfections in the natural order of things — even when they appear beautiful. If there is any uneasiness in re-defining "perfect" as a relative term in order to capture all of our gifts and attributes, then we should add the perfectly human term, "imperfect," with it, and then be perfectly comfortable in so doing. Describing ourselves and others as "perfectly imperfect" is absolutely correct because there isn't any one of us that doesn't fall under this category. After all, if we're not flawed in some way, then we can't truly be like the Persian rug — beautiful.

Accepting Differences

ONE OF THE biggest obstacles in fully implementing the process of acceptance of ourselves as well as others is the resistance, either conscious or unconscious, to relinquish preconceived ideas and beliefs about people, things, and circumstances that stunt our growth. On a worldwide scope, peoples, countries, and governments fight against one another because of their preconceived ideas and beliefs concerning what each other should be doing, believing, or even look like. Ideologies bring divisions instead of national pride, and religions bring hatred instead of spiritual nourishment. Even within the borders of our own country, people are divided because of their differences and beliefs — to the degree of killing one another. If we need a reminder of this bad behavior, we need look no further than our inner cities gangs, with their different colors and ethnic backgrounds, as they kill one another instead of engaging in the difficult process of coming to a mutual understanding. As a species, we sometimes refuse to exit our comfort zones to find a common ground in accepting differences as a healthy and normal part of being a "perfectly imperfect" human race.

On a more personal level, we can develop preconceived ideas about the differences that exist between people. We often shut each other out in order to ensure our safety from an unknown imaginary threat. The opportunities for inner growth are limited as we teach one another that any kind of contact with people that appears to be outside our definition of normality should be avoided. Growth comes when we put aside our fears and have the courage to willingly accept one another's differences. We learn through our willingness that by looking beyond the different skin colors, languages, disabilities, societal status, and traditions that commonalities surface in our humanity. Our fears, disappointments, need for happiness, love and acceptance all have one overriding characteristic — they make up the innermost part of the soul. Each of us is vital in expanding our collective acceptance of one another. The unifying chain of acceptance can be straightened, weakened, or broken depending on how we were taught by our parents and those in charge of nurturing us to adulthood. It is what and how we teach our children that can create within them either a limited or expansive view as they explore the human differences that surround them. We must let them know that acceptance of our humanity has no boundaries. This is the only sure way to increase the amount of peace and love that exists in our world and put an end to hatred and intolerance.

Becoming as a Child

As I was shopping at Wal-Mart, a young child who was holding his mother's hand, looked down at my feet and immediately looked up at me, inquiring with an innocent sincerity, "Mister, why do you walk the way you do?" Welcoming the question, I started to explain to him in a manner that I thought he could understand as to why I walked that way. I was not able to get three words out before his mother verbally scolded him. She told him to leave the poor man alone and to not ask questions. I suddenly realized the poor man she referred to was me! I couldn't believe this, since I hardly considered myself a poor man, and was having a great day! She then apologized for her son's curiosity. I tried to explain to her that I liked it when others openly asked questions. She walked away, holding her child's hand and said, "We teach him better . . . sorry."

While I'm sure she had every good intention in protecting him, as well as me, that mother's reaction to her child's openness may have had a limiting influence on her child's willingness to interact with others that may look different than him — perhaps for the rest of his life! He may now feel more uncomfortable in doing so because, through his experience, he learned that people who are different are unapproachable and any inquiry that he might make will be suppressed out of a fear of offending others. Therefore, instead of breaking these barriers, and expanding his views and acceptance of those around him, he may choose the limited path of non-acceptance, not because of wanting to be cruel or mean to others, but wishing to avoid learned uncertainty that results in the fear of human differences. The lesson we can all learn from little children is to have the courage to make a genuine inquiry and then, once a satisfactory answer is found, move on to the things that truly matter. Once in a while we need to allow childlike instincts to take the lead without grown up interference.

Breaking Free

BY DEVELOPING THE childlike attribute of genuine acceptance, we free ourselves from the emotional bondage of fearing our innate differences. Instead of seeing only perfection existing outside ourselves, we see it internally, existing in our individual characteristics that makes us each truly unique. When we do this, we break out of the prison that we build around ourselves by thinking we're a creature classed in an entirely unknown category of species and sometimes from an entirely different planet because of our differences and personal limitations. True liberation is found only when we accept our uniqueness and creatively adapt.

Self-acceptance is not apathy! Apathy is throwing in the towel and believing that we are absolutely powerless to change and improve our circumstances. Acceptance is the belief that we have the power to move forward, not despite our human differences, but because of them. The time to break free is ours to determine and no one can do it for us. And how do we know when we are liberated from our self-imposed bondage? When we come to the realization that our only real limitations are the ones we impose upon ourselves because of the fear and dread of not fitting into the mold we think we should be able to fit. When we can look into the mirror and say with unwavering confidence that we're willing to be our personal best, without having to be someone else's, we have succeeded.

"Mirror, Mirror on the Wall"

WHILE I WAS attending college, I met a girl who appeared to have cerebral palsy, as I did, but to a lesser degree. We started talking about our long-term goals and aspirations. I made the assumption that she knew that we had our physical disabilities in common. And because I made this assumption, I automatically made another — that it would be safe to discuss the challenges I thought we held in common.

I started out by asking her how long she had had cerebral palsy. I was literally stunned as she started to get very upset, telling me that she absolutely did not have this horrible physical condition. She set me straight that her physical differences were only due to growing adjustments her body was undergoing, and she would surely grow out of this difficult phase in a few years, just as her parents had always assured her.

We dated for a few months and she always appeared quite upset at not knowing why she walked and talked a little different than those around her. Her thoughts were constantly focused on why she was different. These repeated thoughts kept her in a holding pattern where she was unable to have further personal growth. Her academic life and personal relationships suffered, including the one with herself as a result of not fully accepting who she was. Instead of creatively adapting to her situation, and getting the little extra assistance she may have needed to excel in her studies and the rest of her life, she went without in order to prove the point that she was perfect, in the purest sense — a point that not one of us can rationally make.

I finally asked her if it was so horrible that I had cerebral palsy. That would be my last question to her! She angrily told me never speak to her again. About a year later, when I saw her on campus, she apologized for her denial and attitude. She said that she finally accepted the fact she had been living with cerebral palsy. She went on to explain that my interaction with her was like a mirror that was too painful for her to look into.

It was then that I began to relate to her perspective. At one point in my life, I was unable to interact or even look at another disabled person without feeling the inner pain of looking in my mirror and comparing my imperfect self with the perfect world.

While I attended high school, my mother always encouraged me to go on local outings with a group of kids my age who all had some kind of disability. At this stage in my development, I was unwilling to look at that painful reflection and accept myself as such. Instead of condemning my "girlfriend" for her feelings toward me, I remembered what it felt like to be, at one point in my life, behind my own bars of self denial. I was now able to empathize with her while feeling truly grateful to finally be free from the illusionary bondage into which we all put ourselves.

I learned two valuable lessons from that experience. First, I learned that we can't always assume how another person is dealing with a particular situation, even if it does resemble our own, or at what stage of self-acceptance they are. Again, no one can know what it is like to live in our particular reality, with our own set of struggles and hurdles. No matter how much we may want to process others' life situation for them, they must do it for themselves. On the surface, this may seem an unfortunate truth that prompts us never to get out of bed in the morning. To the contrary, it is a truth that reassures us that we have the power for positive change lying at the very core of our "individual" being.

Secondly and more importantly, I also learned that by not being able to accept our particular circumstance or reality, we keep ourselves in a state of emotional bondage. Sometimes our preconceived notions about how life ought to be, instead of how it actually is, are the steel bars that are holding us captive — an illusion that at times we make quite real for ourselves. Asking questions like, "why me?" leads to prolonged incarceration as our minds can only respond with rationalizations for continued victimhood. Questions like, "why not me?" on the other hand, lead to liberation.

It would be a wonderful world if we could all be secure enough within ourselves to get to know and accept one another for who and what we truly are. Inquiries into our diversities should be seen as welcome mats for healthy relationships, instead of an offensive slap in the face. There are still some who get offended with our willingness to be open with them. We can't let the few allow their insecurities to get the best of them, keep us in a state of collective isolation, without the opportunity for inner growth. We need to start assuming that a new level of security and conscious awareness already exists. This new heightened awareness will allow our interactions to be more genuine with one another and that will result in succeeding generations lowering these barriers. Ultimately, self-acceptance is essential for collective acceptance to take hold and it all starts with the power of one.

Freeing Our "Perfect" Vision

LIFE'S ADVERSITY AND challenges can in one instance bring us down yet in the very next instance, we can become empowered with a heightened confidence, knowing that having struggles doesn't mean we have to give up on what we've set out to do. This sudden shift in perspective happens with a willingness to creatively adapt in order to bring into our reality whatever we have set our sights upon. In other words, we hold our vision as real and attainable, and above all, worthwhile. The most difficult part is having the positive self-talk and patience to be able to hold the vision steady in the forefront of our minds — while bridling the temptation to give up. While the latter may be easier, the former is almost certain to bring successful results. The ability to hold on to our vision and then have the ability to manifest it reverberates outward as examples of the incredible power of inner and outer perseverance.

Many of us discount our own visions because we think what we want is insignificant and not worthy of being important. We hold our individual visions hostage to our perception that it must either be big and grandiose to be worthy of our consideration or it is too big and beyond our capability to even manifest itself. So instead of holding onto our visions, as discussed in Chapter 4, we drop them altogether and achieve absolutely nothing! But like the word "perfect," the word "vision" is relative. It is not a one-size-fits-all proposition! If your favorite snack food is a peanut butter and jelly sandwich, and you happen to get an extreme craving at one a.m. and can't get to sleep without having one, then for that moment in time, that becomes your "perfect vision." And yes, it's okay to start manifesting our vision, even if it turns out to look more like a dough ball rather than a sandwich!

The" Perfect" Dough Ball

IT WAS ABOUT one a.m.; I was lying in bed trying to get to sleep when a sudden craving for a peanut butter and jelly sandwich rushed over me like a tidal wave. All I could think about was that sandwich and how delicious it would taste with an ice-cold glass of milk.

I was living alone at the time and had never before made a peanut butter and jelly sandwich; I initially gave up the idea of satisfying my craving — at least for that particular night. But lying there, looking up at the ceiling, I only got hungrier! This gave me the determination to go to the kitchen and at least make an attempt to satisfy my hunger. As I visualized my perfect sandwich, I got the ingredients out of the cupboard: white Wonder Bread and two jars, one containing peanut butter and the other jelly. At that point, my kitchen was perfectly clean. I took a butter knife out of the drawer and stuck it right in the middle of the jar of peanut butter. As I attempted to spread it ever so evenly on the bread, I was unable to get the peanut butter off the knife and onto the bread. Before I knew it, there were pieces of bread scattered across the once-clean counter top. Tiny globs of peanut butter were on each piece of mutilated bread, but most of it went on the ceiling and the walls as my tight, flying, uncoordinated arms involuntarily put them there. Currents of discouragement started overcoming me, feeling sorry for myself, because after all, I couldn't even make my own peanut butter and jelly sandwich. How pathetic!

I decided to throw the entire mess in the trash and go to bed. But wait! I still had the craving and I wanted that sandwich, no matter what it looked like. I started to get enough courage to tackle the jelly. The butter knife went in the jelly and I couldn't keep it on the knife long enough to get it over to the bread, or what was left of it. My arms started flying again and so did the jelly. I finally managed to get the jelly on the little pieces of bread and I now had PB&J wallpaper — but nothing closely resembling the sandwich I had envisioned and wanted.

I was so exhausted and frustrated that I headed for the trash once again, but this time it was for real. I was done with the whole mess. But wait! I still had the craving and by now, I wanted it so bad that I could taste it. Going to bed hungry was no longer an option! After surveying the mess that had been created, I took the pieces with little globs of peanut butter and jelly on each and stuck them all together into a peanut butter and jelly dough-ball. I poured myself a glass of milk, half of which went on the floor. I put the dough-ball on a clean plate and ended up eating the whole thing. And you know what? It was worth every ounce of effort because even though it may not have looked like the sandwich I had originally intended, it tasted as good as I imagined. For me, the peanut butter and jelly dough-ball had been transformed from a nightmarish experience to my "perfect vision."

Innovating Ourselves

WHEN WE INNOVATE something, we expand on it. We stretch its potential to become more of what it was meant to be. This process starts with a seed or idea that sprouts into new technologies or inventions that add something more to the world. A prime example of this is the advent of modern filmmaking, an evolutionary process that first started with the crude looking silent films of the early twentieth century. In less than a few decades, filmmaking evolved and was innovated to create the talking synchronized movies we see today. Gradually, higher quality sound effects and graphics were added to create such films as George Lucas's *Star Wars* — and all in the very same century when just getting "talkies" was considered state-of-the-art.

Star Wars was re-released in the beginning of the twenty-first century, not to change its timeless content, but to expand on what was already considered extraordinary cinematography, with even better special effects and sound. Filmmakers were taking the best and expanding its potential to become even better. In other words, they were innovating!

When we are innovating ourselves, like the film industry, we don't throw away what we already possess and reinvent the wheel; we create and expand and build upon on our unique gifts, talents, and abilities. Just as new technologies are created by expanding the potential from the existing original ones, so we can best expand our own potential by doing the same.

When we excuse ourselves for our humanness, we are sure to put limits on developing our one-of-a-kind "Perfect Circle." We keep on drawing our circle over and over to make it look like everyone else's and in the final analysis, discover that no two ever look alike. The big learning curve begins when we strive for sameness in order to fit into the "in crowd." Our sometimes desperate search to "fit in" to a particular mold is perhaps the most critical step in the process toward individual wholeness — coming full circle with our Perfect Circle. This quest for sameness is most prevalent in our later childhood to adolescent years.

Frequently, the school hallways from elementary to senior high are jam-packed with designer labels that vary from year-to-year and decade-to-decade. Current trends are determined by the group everyone wants to emulate. As mentioned earlier, adolescence is a rite of passage to finding our genuine humanness. After trying to be the same as everyone else, fitting a round peg into a square hole, hopefully we'll learn that this is literally impossible and refrain from our efforts in trying to do so. Our uniqueness will finally be liberated and we won't feel the need to excuse ourselves or say we're sorry for being unable to jam ourselves into a mold that was never intended to be. As a toddler finally learns to walk, so we can learn to fly, discovering our own talents and ways of making a contribution that only we can make. When it's time to take off and we don't, we become subject to the misery of buying into the illusion that our ultimate potential is sameness, when in reality, it's quite the opposite. Sometimes an apology or saying "excuse me" is appropriate when those times come that need legitimate pardoning, but to pardon ourselves for being genuinely human is not only unnecessary but detrimental to our long-term progress toward innovating ourselves.

Excuse Me!

IN TRYING TO fit into the so-called "normal world," I felt undeserving to be allowed. After all, I reasoned, I was dependent on the assistance others would have to offer me to live in such a world. Like all the disabled, I was only a drain on society that I desperately wanted to fit into. I honestly believed everything that fell under the umbrella of the term "perfect" did not include anything having to do with me. It was as if I was trying to be in an exclusive club where I was not qualified to enter. I had to excuse myself for not being like the rest of its members so that "they" might accept me. I wasn't able to wear designer labels to hide my physical differences. I walked and talked differently and could not disguise myself no matter how hard I tried. I was being denied admittance to the exclusive club of "normal people" because I couldn't be one of them. I just couldn't fit the costume "they" mandated I wear. I'll bet you're asking yourself about now, "What is this exclusive club you're referring to?" and "Who are 'they' anyway?" Well, to answer the first question, I formed the club, and in reference to the second, "they" is actually "ME!"

One amazing discovery I've made about negative thinking and self-talk is that it hangs onto us for dear life. Years after thinking I rejected the role of the helpless victim and feeling that I didn't need to excuse myself for being myself, the reality hit me like a ton of bricks that subconsciously, I still was! My family and friends brought to my attention that I needed to delete the word "sorry" from my vocabulary. At first, I thought they were telling me that humility was a sin and we should never admit when we've made a mistake. But they weren't saying that at all. They began to assist me in developing vital insights about my own self-talk by asking me why I frequently said I was sorry. I sounded like I was sorry for everything I did, right down to being alive! I knew this was utterly ridiculous as I knew I had risen above feeling the low self-esteem I had once felt in my past. But that was the past and I no longer felt as if I had to excuse myself for being different or to fit into any particular mold. Of course, I'm fully aware of the apologies I made when it was appropriate, like accidentally stepping on someone's foot or when petitioning for forgiveness from another, but never when it wasn't needed.

The awareness unfolded that I was using the phrase, "I'm sorry" at the expense of my self-worth. Since more than one person brought this to my attention, there must have been some truth there. They were right! While sitting at a restaurant, I said the phrase "I'm sorry" on two occasions after asking the waiter for a refill of ice water. He reminded me that he was being paid to serve, and if patrons didn't need assistance, he would be out of a job. His logic registered and guess what I said next? I was sorry for saying I was "sorry." Like a runaway train, I mentally had to get on the right track and stop the unwarranted series of apologies.

As I became more aware of the pattern, I wanted to stop more than ever, as it made no sense as to why it occurred. I realized that "sorry" when used and abused was the apologetic password to gain admittance into that imagined exclusive club or mold I had years ago created in my mind. I became aware that at one time, I felt a need to apologize for being different in order to be buzzed in to the "normal world" or club. Yes! I felt a need to pardon myself as someone who, in my mind, was a complete menace to society because "sometimes" I would fall down or get food on my face when trying to get it into my mouth. Of course, today I realize that everyone has done these imperfect things.

People who love to eat ice cream and say they have never gotten it on their faces are either unwilling to admit they're perfectly imperfect or they don't eat ice cream. Food servers have jobs because we need another refill of ice water and big companies that manufacture napkins show a profit because of the messes on our faces that we sometime make. As the familiar saying goes, "old patterns are hard to break." And so it is with the pattern of saying "sorry" — when it is totally unnecessary. That habit was only going to release its hold when I realized the last remaining remnants of old insecurities and fears were hanging on for dear life — only to be washed away with the updated awareness that even though they might still be there, in a fleeting thought, they have no practical or real application. **We don't always have to say "excuse me" for being perfectly imperfect!**

My father attended high school with the comedian and actor Steve Martin. After graduating, my father and Steve went to work acting in old-time melodramas at the Bird Cage Theater at Knott's Berry Farm in Southern California. As daily performances became routine, my father recalled how they would find more innovative ways to lure people to watch them perform. It was then that Steve Martin started thinking "outside the box" by developing new ways to make people laugh and they definitely did.

He took the traditional nineteenth century slapstick melodrama one step further by adding his own style of comedy to it. He devised a way to make it appear he had an arrow through his head while doing "wild and crazy" magic tricks. He added his individual genuine uniqueness or "Perfect Circle" to his separate act that followed the main show; or "olio," as it was referred to in old-time entertainment venues.

His career as a renowned comedian and later, actor, took flight from his willingness and yes, even courage to be who he was meant to be — unleashing his innate creativity and talent and being himself. Drawing from his own well of personal innovation resulted in adding to his creative brand of comedy where he later found he could tickle the funny bone of millions just by saying, "**EXCUSE ME!**"

While anyone else who said this might get a second glance to see just what they were excusing themselves for, he generated roars of laughter like only he could. Steve Martin's vision, willingness, and resiliency paid off as he took his new brand of humor to comedy clubs around the country and ultimately to the nationally syndicated television show *Saturday Night Live,* where the arrow through his head and the obnoxious "EXCUSE ME" became a household staple that made us laugh.

The "Wild and Crazy Guy," as he commonly has referred to himself, gives us a valuable pointer on how to truly live. He gives us a demonstration of how we can innovate ourselves by fitting into our own mold and making no apologies for doing so. This world-renowned actor and comedian still entertains us today with movies spanning from comedy to drama. We see him play a variety of characters that are sometimes unexpected because he continues to innovate and build upon the talents he already genuinely possesses. And what is the main ingredient that can be attributed to the success of Steve Martin? He doesn't feel a need to offer apologies for being different and he created a mold that no one else could. In other words, he doesn't need to excuse himself when saying, "EXCUSE ME" — even with an arrow through his head.

The common error many of us make in innovating ourselves is that we believe that to break out of a mold of sameness, we need to fit into another that is equally untended for us. We equate the willingness to be different than the rest with the requirement to go above and beyond the call of duty. The order of the day is to put on a mask, or several of them for that matter, to be able to be like everyone else, or worse yet, put one on because we're ashamed to be ourselves. The quest for sameness becomes so painful that instead of being the same as everyone else, we go to the other extreme and become "anti" this or that to prove we're different and not about to try and fit into another's mold.

If we can't fit into the "in crowd," sometimes we feel a need to turn against the crowd, creating an "in crowd" of our own, trying to get others to join our new brand of sameness. We go out of our way to not excuse ourselves, even when there is legitimate cause to do so. We end up putting arrows through our heads, not to make the world a brighter place with more joy and laughter, as Steve Martin did, but to rebel against the status quo, making sure people know we've risen above societal norms that we feel are impossible for us to fit into. Playing the victim role for any extended amount of time, consciously or unconsciously, makes it easier to believe we really are not only playing it — but actually living it!

I discovered, after transcending my own role as the helpless victim, that I was indeed falling down and slurring my words more often and acting more physically impaired than I actually was during this emotionally turbulent phase of my life. Why did I do this?

As I gained more insight into my behavior during this period, I discovered that as long as I believed I was being excluded from the illusionary club of "normal people" that I created, I might as well play the part well. It was then I decided to join the club that would accept me with open arms, the one with "victim" written all over it. Even though I have a hard time believing it myself, falling down often became my signature! If we're falling down because we can't help it, as I sometimes do, then it becomes included in our "Perfect Circle," but if we're doing it as part of feeling self-pity, then we need to reevaluate our thinking. I learned that my disability was not really who I was and whenever possible, I needed to overcome it.

I look back on this painful period, for both myself and those I love, and wish I could erase it, but I can't! I have sincerely said "I'm sorry" to those I affected as a result of acting like the hopeless victim. We all regret our past actions that occurred as a result of "growing pains." To pardon ourselves is appropriate and a necessary step in moving forward.

Innovating ourselves occurs when we don't feel a need to go out of our way to be different, because we're perfectly comfortable with our own innate differences. We create our lives from the template or mold only we can possess, that no one can duplicate. For us, "thinking outside the box" doesn't mean we have to go out of our way, drawing unnecessary attention to ourselves, being someone we're not; but rather, seeing what is already within that is ready to unfold. For some it might be putting arrows through their heads, making us laugh; for others, it may be getting ice cream on their face more often than getting it into their mouths.

To say "sorry" or "excuse me" does have powerful and edifying applications when we're seeking forgiveness. On the other hand, if we're always pardoning ourselves or saying, "I'm sorry" for not being able to fit into the mold that was never originally intended for us, then we are lagging behind in not being truly innovative.

Conclusion

THERE IS ABSOLUTELY no justification for fearing or shying away from our innate human differences if we can view ourselves and others as being perfectly imperfect. We can all be seen as an authentic Persian rug, with its beauty, one-of-a-kind symmetry, and yes, flaws. We may want our children to be safeguarded from this reality, but in the end, we will impair their ability for individual and collective acceptance. They will only be able to perceive human flaws as something that keeps them from seeing the beautiful patterns of humanity. The difference between an authentic and imitation Persian rug will not be noticed because our children were never taught to accept the flaws that make "the authentic one" clearly stand out from all the rest. And whether or not we like to admit it, we've all had a peanut butter and jelly dough-ball experience of one kind or another. Even if we're in denial about it, we've all, either literally or figuratively, or both, thrown a little peanut butter and jelly around and sometimes made a complete mess. But we shouldn't be ashamed! As long as we can squeeze the pieces of scattered bread together to make a creation that is uniquely ours, then we have become "perfectly imperfect" with a one-of-a-kind rug on which to stand.

Never does a man know the force that is in him till the force of affliction and grief has humanized the soul.
—Frederick W. Robertson

Chapter 9

Looking Beyond Ourselves

I RECALL A time that a friend and I went four-wheeling in the desert. We had some high adventure riding the rough terrain. As the sun was setting and we were heading home, we could see the main highway in the distance. Somehow we missed the turn onto the dirt road that led back to civilization. The temperature had significantly dropped and we had no coats or blankets to keep warm. Deep impassable chasms kept us from going where we wanted to go. After about three hours of driving around with no success, we resigned ourselves that we would have to wait for sunrise to find the small road back. Even though our lives weren't in danger, we felt some apprehension about being in the desert in the dark and cold of the night. Once familiar surroundings quickly became unfamiliar! I felt a sense of heaviness and fear as I anticipated the long night ahead.

As we parked, something prompted us to make one last attempt by backtracking, carefully following our tire tracks back where we had been. The amazing thing was that we both felt that if we did this carefully, we would be successful. We went back with headlights' high beams guiding our way through the darkness. What was once an expansive desert landscape, where we could see for miles, was now one where we could only see what was directly in front of us. We slowly retraced our tracks and came upon a brown post that marked the small dirt road we were so desperately trying to find. As we began to see familiar surroundings, the lightness and sense of adventure we felt earlier returned. The lights of the city were a welcoming sight. The next morning, we perceived the situation quite differently than we had the night before when we were in the thick of it. We were able to see the experience as something that added to our exciting adventure.

This experience brings to mind the times in our life's journey when change and loss happen. This could be the death of a loved one, getting older, or transitioning from one position or situation to the next — feeling a sense of grief and loss for what used to be.

When we feel thrown off the beaten path, and lose our bearings of the familiar, we feel the darkness or grief that leaves us feeling stranded and empty inside. Deep chasms form in the soul that prevents us from feeling whole again — as what we have lost becomes our missing piece. It is then we have a space or void left within that longs to be filled. And like being in the lonely desert night, we want to find the road back home. Of course we want our deceased loved ones to return, or whatever once gave us comfort and security to be restored to its original state. But the hard facts of life are that change happens and no matter how hard we try, we can't stop it. So what can we do with the undesired emotion of grief to benefit us in completing our "Perfect Circle?"

First, we must accept the reality that change is the one constant and that the "perfectly imperfect" human, yes, that means you and I, can be very resistant to it. We should expect to have the "empty void" when it occurs. We can't judge ourselves because we grieve in times of loss, especially over a loved one. If we are able to find human beings that claimed to never have been affected by some kind of change or loss in their lives, we can safely assume they have either taken up full-time residence in a cave, with their own shadow as their only friend, or are in a complete state of denial. So for the record, as with all adversity, grief is not something to avoid like some abnormality or sickness, but rather, is a healthy part of life. We should not judge or put a rigid timetable on this painful emotion.

Secondly, we need to summon the technology of the human spirit by asking ourselves a simple but most profound question, "What am I learning from this experience?" It is then we need to be patient for the answer that will be different for everyone, but with the common theme of the need to look beyond ourselves. When we do this, we feel the pain and emptiness of our loss, and then move not only through it, but beyond it by answering the call to do something more that requires us to travel into an unknown territory. We are called to embrace our feelings of grief by seeing it in the broader context of learning something more that ennobles us about ourselves and those around us. New awakenings surface and inner foundations are strengthened. Like all adversity, the void within was created out of normal human encounters with loss and change and can be used as a tool for our continued growth and inward expansion. If we feel at home when learning and growing, no matter how uncomfortable or unfamiliar it becomes, we will never leave the "welcoming mat" of our front door.

The Void that Tugs

The uncomfortable changes that happen in our lives can often force us to broaden the scope of our reality. As a social worker, I often saw the death of a family member providing those left behind with the opportunity to move beyond themselves by redefining who they were in relationship to those around them. Siblings and other family members reconcile their differences and come to realize the importance of being fully present with one another, giving their mutual support during this difficult period. Survivors of change and loss get an opportunity to develop a heightened sense of empathy and compassion as they explore uncharted dimensions of their humanity. Grief is the emotion that tugs and pulls us from what we have always known — into the unknown. Like getting off the trail, this can be very uncomfortable and unnerving, until we get our bearings, going forward in a life that is now different and will continue to be so.

Those caring for their terminally ill loved ones, and then losing them, discover the compassion and drive to reach out in ways they never knew they could. The intense pain of their own loss pushes them into having more empathy and awareness for others. Changing roles, such as losing a job or having our children go away to college, can lead the way for strengthening our inner foundations. We come to realize it is these challenges that make it possible to recognize strengths we never knew we had. And as in Plato's cave allegory, we can move beyond the shadows on the walls and begin to see things as they really are, as opportunities for our inward personal expansion.

No longer do we mistake the darkness of the shadows for our reality in place of the light of the sun. Being stuck in our feelings of fear and loss may mean a temporary period of maturation, getting ready to emerge with a vision of opportunity with the capacity to see beyond ourselves and our suffering. It is the polarity between the darkness of the cave and the light outside that makes the brightness of the sun recognizable. In this case, we begin to see flux and change as an essential part of our life's purpose. No longer are the soul's chasms, created by loss and change, seen as impassable, but as one of life's greatest teachers, as we take an alternative route to higher ground — only to feel the power and ever-widening capacity of the human spirit. It is then, as we look back, we come to know that the rough terrain just traversed was not traveled in vain.

Every time there is a change in our lives, there is something that dies and something that is born. Life is a series of cycles that provide us a need to reevaluate our beliefs about who we are and who we are meant to become. We grieve during these periods as we realize that outdated beliefs and life patterns need to be surrendered to adopt new ones that are essential to move forward. Insecurities are challenged and need to be dropped, making room for new and long-needed securities to come to the forefront. We must let go of what is holding us back, moving through the uncomfortable transition moments from the known into the unknown and back again. Losing our insecurities and low self-esteem can be like the death of a friend that has enabled us to avoid taking the risk of being all we were meant to be. We grieve for the safety and security we once had by having to say farewell to the need for constant external validation and approval. No matter how painful our loss, we are pushed beyond ourselves to rely upon our inner wisdom and knowledge. This builds enduring foundations that we can stand on with confidence and a new-found purpose that is awaiting the old to pass and the new to be born.

Grieving to our Potential

I REMEMBER MY first experience of losing something close to me. It occurred when I started attending high school and realized that I was different! Although I had my disability from birth, now comparing my abilities to others in this new world made it seem that a piece of me was missing. The second loss or death happened when I graduated with an undergraduate degree in political science and realized I was now officially an adult and had to rely on my inner wisdom. In simpler terms, I had to grow up and stop relying on others to validate me. Seeking external approval was like an old friend holding me up by the bootstraps.

In growing up with a physical disability, I didn't see myself having the same boyhood experiences as those around me. Although I had the same interests, my opportunities were different. I was unable to rough it up on dirt bikes as I saw others doing. I realized that my opportunities for dating would be different as people may have to take more time getting to know me and become more comfortable with someone having a physical disability. The image I had of myself was that I did not meet society's expectations of a "real man." I thought a law career would more than compensate for what I was physically lacking. I had adopted the erroneous belief that becoming a lawyer would, without a doubt, create an alpha male or "macho" image. When I started my undergraduate studies in political science at the University of Nevada, Las Vegas, my goal was to go to law school — to complete myself. But first, I needed external validation to make certain my feelings and decisions were correct.

I did everything I could do to earn the "rite of passage" to become a "real man" in society. The day of my graduation came and went, and so did the days of not trusting and believing in myself. I was fortunately faced with one incident that would force me to build my self-reliance. I sought counsel and wisdom from two people I held in high esteem. Everything they counseled me to do, I did! I assumed they were always right, including matters of my prospective law career. However, this time they didn't agree.

I now stood alone, with my future and self-esteem in the balance. One of them validated my erroneous belief that becoming a lawyer would definitely turn me into a real man. The other thought my physical limitations would make it impossible to pursue such a career. It felt as if the bottom had just dropped out from under me as my old friend, or external validation that I had grown accustomed to, was gone. My void was formed. There I was, left alone to do something for myself that I was not used to doing, validate myself by relying on my inner wisdom to make my own decisions.

I discovered that I was going after a law career for all the wrong reasons; and, after all, it really wasn't my passion. I knew I needed to take the first step and go in a different direction and rely on myself for the answers. And yes, the person that believed I needed to be a lawyer to become a "real man" had nothing to do with me after I made my decision to go another direction. Oh, the growing pains!

I asked myself what my true aspirations were and the answers showed up. No, there was not a sudden gigantic personal revelation where my complete life map was laid out with every direction pinpointed. The answers and opportunities came gradually as I became more receptive to them. As mentioned earlier, I have always felt a strong need to help people who were dealing with their own physical adversities. What was so different about this desire from the one of wanting to pursue a law career?

The only difference was that this desire came from the genuine knowledge and wisdom about who I was and wanted to become as a result of my life experiences, instead of the fear of not measuring up. In other words, it came from the accumulated wisdom of the soaring human spirit instead of the ego's "fight or flight" response.

I received an unexpected phone call from the volunteer coordinator at the Las Vegas-based Nathan Adelson Hospice to speak to a group of his volunteers. He heard about me through a mutual acquaintance at the university. He requested that I speak specifically about how the care and compassion provided by others helped me live with a disability. This topic was appropriate since these were the people who would give their time, without financial gain, to assist the terminally ill and their families. I was totally dumbfounded by the invitation because I didn't think my life experiences were good enough to tell anyone — much less an entire group of volunteers. The transition from lawyer to speaker was difficult, but well worth it!

After speaking to these volunteers, I realized that they all had been led to assist the terminally ill because of their own life adversity experiences. I was amazed to hear that many of them had stories of losing their loves ones which, in turn, heightened their sense of compassion, driving them to look and then reach beyond themselves. No matter what their circumstances, they all expressed the same inner need to reach out, using the hospice as a vehicle toward that end. And yes, there were "real men" who felt this way, and were in the class! My presentation went surprisingly well and for the first time, the direction I would take began to become clear.

The *Road & Track* magazine was put away and I picked up a copy of Elisabeth Kubler-Ross's renowned book, *On Death and Dying*. I read it from cover to cover! What amazed me most was not how I could help the terminally ill, but how much they would be able to teach me with their own wisdom and knowledge as they approached the end of their lives. I became so excited about this "soul expanding feeling" that I enrolled in the next hospice volunteer training course. Helping these people was a voyage in self-discovery. They were the best examples of how to show gratitude and above all let go and allow life's processes to unfold — something in which I desperately needed instruction at the time. Little by little, I learned to let life unfold as it should and it did. I volunteered in hospice for over a year and found the experience as enriching as I originally had anticipated.

I started receiving calls by word-of-mouth to speak to various organizations around Las Vegas. I ended up speaking professionally to various student leadership groups around the country. I was also hired for two years as a sensitivity speaker for the human resource department at the MGM Grand Hotel in Las Vegas. This allowed me the opportunity to teach thousands of their employees how to extend genuine acceptance and sensitivity to millions of their visitors who have their own human differences.

Social work became a clear career choice for me to continue my passion of helping others. My life has continued to unfold as I am willing to let go of my erroneous beliefs and expectations of what I ought to be and accept who I am. As old insecurities are in need of being eulogized, the new securities are born to fill the void. The adjustment or grieving period may be uncomfortable as we enter a new level of self-confidence, but it is worth the effort. Sometimes all we need to do to move forward is to get out of our own way.

Filling the Void

FILLING THE VOID created by life changes can be very uncomfortable as we are required to step beyond what we have always known. When we do this, we grow and expand beyond who we are. We step out of a pattern that we've had for perhaps years into a new and unfamiliar one, one that is not necessarily better, but is of equal importance to our long term growth.

The grieving process takes time, especially if we have lost a loved one and are trying to get over the initial phase of not having them with us. Everyone goes through this process in their own unique way, with some similarities. For instance, we will hear people say they are doing fine and in the next moment, they become quite emotional. We also often hear people say that as they are grocery shopping, a particular item will remind them of their deceased loved one and bring on a wave of emotion.

Another similarity I've observed is how guilt becomes one of the biggest barriers in being able to grow from loss and change. In practicing bereavement counseling, I discovered one of the common themes that exists is the feeling that to get on with their lives would somehow mean they were trying to forget about their loss. In other words, the profound question, "how can I grow from change" translates to, "how can I get this person off my mind?" Many people feel that healthy grieving primarily involves staying isolated, crying uncontrollably with a box of Kleenex in one hand and a picture of their loved ones in the other, thinking their lives can't go on without them. Make no mistake; this is definitely a phase in healthy grieving, but certainly does not encompass it in its entirety.

Another vital phase in the grieving process is when we decide it's time to move beyond the pain. We memorialize those we hold dear by hanging their pictures on the wall, where they are clearly seen, and then take action to look beyond the suffering. When the time is right, mourning will transform itself into a celebration, not only of our life, but the lives of those who have passed before us. We recognize that our emptiness or the void can be replaced by a willingness to move forward as a way of keeping our cherished memories immortalized. After all, in most of the great religions and wisdom traditions of the world, death is seen as going beyond this life in whatever fashion to become more of what we were meant to be. If those we love are able to look and go beyond themselves by dying, why can't we do the same in this life? Consider the possibilities! Grief is good when we allow it to be a process of personal transformation to reach beyond ourselves irrespective of the difficulty.

Good Grief!

MARY WAS A 78-year-old woman whom I had the privilege to observe as she transformed her life through the pain and suffering of change and loss after her husband passed away. For a year prior to his death from lung cancer, she had been his 24/7 caregiver. They had a successful marriage for 56 years, with one daughter, who was supportive of her mother, yet was not able to help her overcome her severe depression from the loss.

Mary was referred to me by her physician who was quite concerned about her prolonged depressed emotional state. When I first contacted her for bereavement counseling, her spouse had been gone for over a year. I discovered Mary had been so stricken with grief she was emotionally paralyzed to the point of being unable to get out of bed in the morning. She isolated herself and was so absorbed in her loss that she started losing contact with those she loved. Most of those people, she said, were sick and tired of hearing repeats of her sob stories. The fascinating thing about Mary was that she had the insight that she was holding herself in a pattern where growth was not possible. Even with this realization, she absolutely refused to engage herself in any bereavement counseling or support groups to initiate positive movement in her life. She didn't want to rehash her pain or hear anyone else's since hers was already bad enough. The ironic point was that she would rehash her issues with anybody who would give her their ear. Her excuse was that her grief was different and no one would understand. Isn't this the reasoning we all at times use, feeling we're alone in our experiences? She was at the threshold of wanting to exit Plato's cave — but couldn't. What was the barrier that was keeping her from the light? Changing her external conditions did not change what was going on inside her. After working with Mary for six months, helping to improve her financial situation and getting her a weekly housekeeper to assist her with errands and cleaning, she still woke up with feelings of hopelessness and abandonment. Her old tune never harmonized with her need to grow beyond herself. I asked how she was benefiting by remaining stuck in her current emotional state. She believed that looking at his picture, while crying all day, demonstrated her love and devotion and to move on would diminish these feelings. In her mind, "textbook" grieving involved only misery and isolation and did not have anything to do with interpersonal growth.

I worked with Mary for over a year and there were no changes in her emotional state. I asked if her husband was alive, what would he want her to be doing and feeling? Her immediate response was that he would want her to be happy and move forward. Slowly, Mary made small changes in her routine, like getting out of bed earlier, eating even when she didn't feel like it, and getting cleaned up for the day ahead. She started playing solitaire again and began attending a bereavement support group with a neighbor who had recently lost her husband. After making these alterations, Mary started verbalizing that she was feeling optimistic and could continue her journey.

I now saw that she was seeing the light shining from the entrance of her cave. She came to the comforting realization that she was not the only person suffering from a loss and was not alone. As she began to be more at ease with expressing her feelings in her bereavement support group, she found that others could help her by sharing their experiences and she could in turn help them by doing the same. Yes, fear that she would forget and stop loving her beloved husband still occupied her mind, but these beliefs were gradually invalidated as she found her most cherished memories of him did not fade as she moved forward.

With the gift of time, she found herself helping others by volunteering as a senior companion. She innovated herself by expanding on her partially correct "textbook" definition of grief by seeing it with new eyes. For Mary, the grieving process not only included a phase of profound sadness, but also one where she was able to use these emotions as a catalyst to look beyond her immediate suffering and make a positive difference in herself and others. Both of these phases of "good grief," however painful, are a healthy and "perfect" part of life. If viewed side by side, they can be used as tools for our fortification and transformation. After all, if her husband would have wanted her to move forward and be happy, why wouldn't she want these same things for herself?

Compassion is the Healer

EVEN THOUGH IT is quite a stretch, when we're able to view loss and change through new eyes, it is transformed from something unbearable into a tool that can be used for our growth. We begin to recognize there is something more to our existence that goes beyond seeing life as a series of events with the only option being to grit our teeth and endure.

With each event, no matter how painful or tragic, there is a hidden gift to be found that facilitates a heightened awareness of humanity and our important part in humanity. It's in these difficult times of painful loss and grief that our human spirit will not only be there to comfort us, but it will take control as it lifts us to discover our capacity to show genuine compassion and humility. The oneness we share with one another is immortalized as our pain and grief is allowed to be the link in the chain called love and compassion, which binds us together.

Living a Compassionate Legacy

ANOTHER REMARKABLE STORY of transformation, through the emotion of grief, was told to me by another client who had recently lost her 42-year-old son to the AIDS virus. She remained very close to him throughout his life and explained how much compassion he showed to all with whom he came in contact.

Eight years earlier, her son was diagnosed with the virus. He then began to volunteer much of his time and energy to both educate people about the virus and lobby in behalf of those who were suffering with it. Throughout the remainder of his life, he fought to prevent and ease the suffering of others, while paying little attention to his own suffering.

Although she misses her son, she knows he died with dignity and was able to fulfill his life's mission in helping others. Through his own encounter with adversity, new avenues opened to satisfy the innermost desires of his heart and to make a difference in this world.

His mother channeled her grief by continuing her son's compassionate legacy. She filled the void in her life by giving her time and energy to carry on his work by speaking and educating others about the AIDS virus. While she still has her moments of extreme sadness and times when she feels sorry for herself, she has managed to maintain feelings of overriding peace and joy knowing she has a connection to him by looking beyond herself. She says, with a strong inner knowing, "I feel as though I never really lost my son as he will always be with me."

Conclusion

ALL OF US will inevitably be confronted with loss and change. We will feel as if we've gotten off our familiar road and chasms block our way back. We will need to stop and survey the landscape to successfully move forward to locate the trail markers pointing the way to higher ground.

We may be scared and lost, with feelings of grief and uncertainty; but these are the scenes of our lives that force us to look beyond ourselves to grow in areas where we never thought we could. The key is to remember it's not what happens to us, it's what we do about it! The emotions of grief and despair all have a season and reason to be in our lives and we can never be fully relieved of them; unless, of course, we want to retreat to the nearest cave. We must remember that these difficult seasons are the invitations for growth and a catalyst for our transformation. These are our opportunities to spread our wings, exiting our cave of shadows, to see the light appearing brighter than it was before we entered.

He that cannot forgive others, breaks the bridge which he must pass himself; for every man has need to be forgiven.

—LORD HERBERT

Chapter 10

Clearing the Way

LIVING IN LAS Vegas during the 1990s, I was able to observe the many older resort hotels as they were demolished to make room for the new multi-million-dollar ultra lavish mega-resorts. It was truly spectacular to see the huge buildings that had for so long been cemented into the town's colorful history come tumbling down in plumes of dust and smoke. Many longtime residents protested the changes to their once small desert oasis. But the big corporations saw that despite the history that would vanish, change was necessary to compete for the tourist dollar. The old had to be destroyed, clearing the way for the new. And whether or not you agreed with it, as the old came down, what went in its place offered not only more to the tourist and industry moguls, but expanded the entire Las Vegas economy — offering more financial opportunity.

Just as large parcels of land along the famous Las Vegas Strip were cleared away to make room for the new skyline, so can we clear our lives for that same reason. Each of us comes into this world, like the land, with clearings in which to build our lives with experiences. Our lives are an accumulation of challenges and interactions with others that will afford us those experiences that will facilitate personal growth. And just as buildings occupy a skyline, our beliefs, expectations, and judgments built from past associations occupy our minds. It is therefore sometimes necessary to bring in the wrecking crew to clear the way for something more expansive in our lives, as what we have built for ourselves may be holding us back. The ability to allow ourselves to forgive and be forgiven is the most effective wrecking crew when it is time to make room for new and more innovative structures or relationships.

Strengthening Relationships

THE RELATIONSHIPS WE have with others, whether family, friends, work related or any other association, give us the finest tutoring in learning such vitally important attributes as love, trust, patience, and selflessness. As we are put into those situations where we can make the choice to freely give of ourselves, we are given the opportunities to cement these attributes into the textures of our being. The experiences discussed in this book focus on one important aspect of our lives, our relationships — with others as well as ourselves. Therefore, the one attribute we should acquire above all others is the ability to forgive and to be forgiven.

The power of forgiveness clears our lives to make space for healthier interactions that facilitate growth instead of stagnation, and peace instead of contention. When we forgive, and allow ourselves to be forgiven, we open the portal to the soul that allows love and acceptance into our life. Ultimately, that will bring pure joy.

Pure joy comes when we see the good all around us, as discussed in Chapter 6, not because of anything possessed or necessarily special in our lives, but just because life itself seems worth all its time and effort. We feel lighter, and each moment is something to be cherished rather than tolerated because we have relieved ourselves of life's unnecessary baggage of guilt, burdens, and resentments. In a sense, when we hold these feelings within ourselves, a dam is created, keeping back those

intentions and interactions that can bring us joy and contentment —
instead of hatred and uneasiness. We must always be in the state of
evaluating the need for demolition or implosion in order to rebuild
something new so we can restart the flow of pure joy. Forgiving the
arch enemy, ourselves, is imperative if we expect to forgive others. It
starts from within.

Arch Enemy #1

MANY OF US don't know where to begin this process or identify the
source of our emotional pain. In reflecting back on the adolescent
and young adult years of my life, I have come to realize that much
of my emotional discomfort came from not forgiving myself for
being born with a disability. Yes, as crazy and ridiculous as this may
sound, I resented myself for not being able to fit in and do the things
I saw others doing. My perceived imperfections and flaws became
arch enemy number one that I needed to finally forgive. Learning
the destructive habit of self-ridicule may have had its origins in the
simple non-acceptance of those imperfectly round tires of the child-
hood race car drawings as discussed in Chapter 1. In other words, I
was not able to complete my "Perfect Circle" early on because the
resentment I had toward myself would not allow that to be.

The pattern continued to worsen as I grew older, preventing true
inner peace and pure joy from being allowed into my life. Every
day was like waking up in a war zone. My external world couldn't
have been better. I had two loving parents who were able to emo-
tionally and physically support me in whatever I wanted to do or
become with food on the table and a roof over my head. Because
my resentment turned inward, toward something about myself, I
could not change and I was unable to see the good part of my life. It
was only after realizing I needed to accept and forgive my disability
and the challenges that accompanied it that I was able to move on
with my life in a positive direction. This did not mean that I had to

somehow learn to celebrate being in a disabled body. Rather, I had to surrender my hostility and the resentment I felt toward it, and learn to love myself, while realizing that the true inner-me could in fact rise above any adversity and challenge that was put before me. Although my disability was indeed a part of me, it was not the true me. The real war was being waged on the inside, not the outside. When I forgave not only my disability but myself for having been born with cerebral palsy, the once heavily contaminated toxic war zone started to clear away to make room for the construction project of inner peace and pure joy.

There were times I came across individuals who weren't as under-standing of my disability as I would have expected them to be. During my adolescence and young adult life, I became judgmental of people whom I thought didn't properly understand me. I was confronted by them on a daily basis without understanding why. I wasn't magically pulling these people into my experience of reality like a rabbit out of a hat, but rather, I was unfairly pulling them into my own negative world by how I perceived myself.

Quite simply, we shape our experience of reality by where we put our focus. During these difficult stages of my development, I thought of myself as a pathetic individual that didn't fit in. So guess what? Reality followed the belief. I vividly recall one occasion when I noticed that, for whatever reason, one particular person started looking at me differently. However, in reality, in this instance there were over fifty people looking at me. My faulty logic was that I began to condemn them all as insensitive individuals without the heart to understand a person with a disability. Looking back, there may have been people looking out of curiosity, but there was really only one person looking at me that perceived me as a pathetic human being, and that insensitive person was "ME!"

The relationships we develop with others are dependent on the one we develop within ourselves. When turmoil and resentment turns inward, we project these hostile feelings outside us to the people with whom we associate. I have observed that our inner world does in fact reflect our outer one. After all, how can anyone understand and accept us unless we are doing the same for ourselves? Forgiving ourselves is the first step in forgiving others. When we do this, we begin to see all of our relationships, including the one we have with ourselves, from the perspective of mutual growth and human understanding.

Understanding the "Understanding" of Others

IN MY LIFE, the acceptance of who I am as well as the disability I live with has given me the clarity to better understand other perspectives. Whether or not people were actually treating me badly or disrespectfully because of my disability was not the issue. The real issue was my own perception of myself. I needed to stop expecting respect from others, and instead, demand it from myself.

Eastern tradition dictates that people greet each other by bowing before them, not to show submissiveness to authority, but rather to show respect and acknowledge the highest or divine state that innately resides within each person. Though we have no such tradition in the West, perhaps we should learn to recognize the divine state of others, and further, we should acknowledge and respect this in ourselves.

A transformation gradually occurred to me as I became willing to forgive others for their sometimes less than accurate perception and ideas of someone who was physically disabled. This does not mean that I approached these people telling them I forgave them for what I thought they either did or did not do. But rather, I changed my perspective by developing a deeper empathy of their personal experiences that formed their current understanding of physically disabled people. I had to surrender my expectations of how I thought others should or ought to act toward me by coming to the realization that they too were on the same path of learning and trying to understand and absorb the world around them just as was I. The fact that they didn't understand my disability the way I did, didn't make them cruel or stupid, but more akin to someone who didn't have knowledge in that particular area. It was my responsibility to not react negatively or judge them, but to understand that they may not know how to react to someone with a physical disability — because it may be their first time in so doing.

Perhaps if I were to judge or react negatively toward them for not behaving or acting as I expected them to, their association with me or someone with a physical disability would have just perpetuated any fears or apprehensions they may have had. The healing power of forgiveness can only be activated if we can allow ourselves to view another's perspective without condemnation or hasty judgment — allowing room for growth and mutual understanding.

The Glowing Understanding

WHEN I WAS 34, I went with my family to a Denny's coffee shop for Saturday morning breakfast. Upon entering the restaurant, I couldn't help but notice they were offering a green glow ball as a promotional item to all the kids who came with their parents. I thought how great it would be to be a kid again and be able to get all the great toys whenever they were offered. As I was now well into my adult years, I surrendered my childhood longing and sat down to eat. The waitress came to take our orders and when it became my turn, she kindly asked my father what I wanted to eat. At first, I wanted to check to see if I was invisible, but instead, I interjected and placed my order. After finishing our meal, she came back with a green glow ball, saying as she handed it to me, "And here you go sweetheart; this is for you." At first, I didn't know if I should jump up and down with excitement or tell her how ignorant she was for treating me like a child. Fortunately for both of us, I did neither, because at this stage in my life, I had shifted my perspective. I was aware of the possibility that maybe she had limited interactions with people who had physical disabilities and was accommodating me the best way she knew how.

Instead of embarrassing her, I replied with the statement of how great it was to be an adult and still get the toys. A little touch of humor can go a long way in breaking down attitudinal barriers that can exist between two people having two totally different types of life experiences. The group at our table started laughing and the waitress joined in. She began to feel more comfortable with the situation as she inquired how I became disabled. As briefly as I could, I explained how and why I had cerebral palsy. Sure enough, she said that she had had very little involvement with people with physical disabilities and she needed to know more about them.

There was no need for apologies as this was a moment of learning and understanding. There was no need to forgive this person, as I had already gone through the process of forgiving the human race, myself included, for not always having the understanding or knowledge that I expected them to have. A rather large part of this process is to take into consideration that we are all part of the same continuum of learning about and experiencing the world. This was not about getting a green glow ball toy and being treated like a child, but about gaining the glowing understanding of one another and allowing growth to occur.

Death: The Great Teacher

NO MATTER WHAT our spiritual orientation or belief is in the afterlife, we all would have to agree that death is the ultimate conclusion for at least this world or experience. Those who are near death have a deeper appreciation for life and have the chance to take a crash-course to learn the vital importance of forgiveness. One of the gifts of assisting and working with the terminally ill and their families is to see how the process of forgiveness can transform not only those making their exit from this world, but also those left behind.

Dorothy's Parting Gift

WHILE WORKING AS a social worker at an inpatient hospice facility, I had the opportunity to work with a 58-year-old woman by the name of Dorothy. She was given about three weeks to live due to a diagnosis of end-stage lung cancer. The first time I introduced myself to her, she became very angry and threw me out of her room for no apparent reason. In finally getting to know Dorothy, I found she also had a heart laden with guilt and remorse. She felt she had been a terrible mother and a poor example of a human being. She had divorced and severed contact with her 16-year-old son and had not seen nor heard from him in ten years. Feeling estranged from her only child became even more emotionally painful now that she was going to die. She felt he had not forgiven her for the past. This guilt overrode her fear of pending death as she felt an urgent need to resolve this family issue before passing on. Dorothy continued living past her expected time by six additional weeks. She got weaker by the day, but repeatedly reassured me she was not going to leave this life or have peace until she could be sure her son had forgiven her for abandoning him, and he knew that she loved him.

As time passed, Dorothy became a kinder person. She opened up her soul to me, telling me that she only wished she could have another chance to relive her life as she was not proud of it. She wanted to make things right before it was over. Intuitively, I felt that if Dorothy could write to her son and tell him how much she loved him and was sorry for any past mistake, then maybe she would be able to acquire enough peace within to be able to move forward with the rest of her journey.

One day, I suggested to her that she write a brief letter to her son telling him how much she loved him. I was quite certain that Dorothy would never do such a thing, especially since she appeared to be quite embittered. I expected her to throw me right out of her room for even making such a suggestion. Surprisingly I was wrong. When

I made the suggestion, Dorothy's face lit up like a firecracker. She immediately directed me to get a box from under her hospital bed. Contained in the box was a package of about fifteen note cards, each with a beautifully painted nature scene.

With all the strength she could muster, she told me that her very close friend had hand painted each card and she was saving them for something special. In an excited voice, she stated, "Now I know exactly what that something special is." She asked me to leave as she wanted time to gather her thoughts to write her son. Given her weakened condition, it took her about two days to complete the letter which I later mailed for her. She was extremely hopeful that somehow her son's heart would soften, forgiving her past mistakes and that she in turn would have the ability to forgive herself.

Two week later, Dorothy's condition worsened and her son did finally come to see her. After his visit, she seemed to be more at peace than I had ever seen her before. A few days after her son's initial visit, Dorothy went into a comatose state with labored breathing. The doctors and nurses told me that she would be dead in a matter of hours and to notify any family members who desired to say their final goodbye.

I called her son to ask him if he wanted to see his mother as she was in her last stage of life. At 3:43 p.m., I was paged over the facility intercom to come to room 410, Dorothy's room. My heart started pounding as I knew this would be the first experience I would actually have being with a person who was in the final stage of dying. As one might imagine, I was quite apprehensive.

As I entered her room, I saw her peacefully lying there with her son holding her hand. I told him I would give them their privacy but would stay nearby. He motioned me with his hand to come in as his mother would want me there. At exactly 5:21 p.m., Dorothy made her passing with her son holding her hand, as he repeatedly told her how much he loved her.

For me, this event seemed almost surreal, but one of the most intimate and sacred moments humans could share. If one had to describe such a feeling, you wouldn't be able to because it defies all human description. I can only say that at that moment, it felt as if time stood still as the healing balm of love and forgiveness was able to be applied to the emotional wounds between a mother and her child, bringing them together again.

A real miracle had just happened as both Dorothy and her son were able to move forward because of her parting gift that was offered that day — the healing power of forgiveness. They both received something of great value by coming to a higher understanding of both themselves and each other.

Initiating the Process

OFTEN, WE NEVER forgive or allow ourselves to be forgiven because the process is never initiated. We wait for the other to make the first move, keeping both parties away from the awesome connecting power that forgiveness has to offer. And like building a bridge, someone has to be the first to get the steel support beams to begin the process. No, it won't always reach to the other side and we may only be able to travel midway as the other party refuses to build their part. It takes courage to take the first step. We face possible rejection and we have to be willing to move beyond our expectations and personal judgments of what should and should not happen. Doing our part in initiating the process may not always bring the exact results we want. If we are sincere in our intent we can not help but be healed or gain some much needed closure. We need to extend the invitation for people to come our way.

Recognizing the "Perfect Circle" that we create for ourselves is the most vital part of bridge building. We have to extend allowances for human error, growing from it, and then make the needed adjustments to move forward. In returning to the theme of the interchangeable roles of the teacher and the student, there has to be a willingness to build our part of the bridge called forgiveness.

Building a Bridge

ONE OF THE most amazing facets of life is how we all, in one way or another, are confronted with the opportunities to learn how to forgive and be forgiven. To observe this process between two outside family members in a professional capacity is one thing, but to experience it with one of your own family members is quite another. It's as if this particular issue has been written into life's curriculum for everyone that has ever lived because it is so imperative for our continued growth. People and circumstances come into our life's path in order to teach us something about the healing power of forgiveness. Timing and circumstances will vary, but like it or not, they will always show up. One such individual came into my life when I was six years of age. He taught us both something of the healing power of forgiveness some thirty-five years later.

It was an ordinary school day and all of the children were playing and having fun as do all normal first graders. I remember Mrs. Hildum, the school principal, walking into our classroom to introduce a new student. She introduced him as David Stewart. I recall thinking how neat it was to share the same last name despite the difference in spelling. David was in a wheelchair and later we were told that he had spina bifida, a physical disability caused by a spinal defect at birth that resulted in him having no feeling below the waist. His disability did not matter. What did stand out in our young minds about David was the fact that he had been abandoned by both of his parents and lived in a convalescent center as a ward of the state. We couldn't help but notice that he came to school with tattered clothes and holes in the knees of his pants.

As the days went by, David and I became the best of friends. It didn't matter if we were on the playground or in the classroom — we were inseparable. About a year went by before I asked my parents if we could take him on one of our outings to Disneyland and a sleepover. They approved and the two of us had the most fun together that we thought we could ever have.

Upon taking David home to the convalescent center, we found that he was the only resident there who wasn't severely mentally retarded. I realized how fortunate I was to have my family that loved me. Before that, I had taken this gift, my parents, for granted.

My mother's compassionate heart was broken after seeing the shattered life of the ten-year-old boy. Her feelings of empathy were so strong that it resulted in her taking action — an action that would change all of our lives forever. She was so determined to change David's life for the better that without giving a second thought, she went home and started making plans to take him as one of her own. I couldn't believe that my best friend would now be my brother.

As soon as David became a permanent part of our family, for some unknown reason, our close relationship ended. The harder I tried to rekindle our once close schoolmate friendship, the more estranged we became. When I tried to talk to him or ask him if he wanted to do some fun activity together, David would tell me that he wanted to be left alone. As the months and years passed, I lost all hope that we would ever be friends, let alone best friends, ever again.

Resentment toward him built inside me as I couldn't understand what had caused our now mutual estrangement. I felt that if it had not been for me, this once-abandoned soul wouldn't have had the remotest chance to be part of a real family. Because of this, I felt that David owed it to me to make reconciliation and be my friend, no matter what it took. My resentment toward him inflated to such a degree that eventually I didn't care what happened in his life. Even after hearing that his best friend in high school had taken his own life by jumping from a busy freeway overpass, I had to pretend to care how this must have impacted David. My feelings toward my once best friend turned into hatred that I allowed to fester well into my middle adult years.

When David was 38 and I was 36, his physical health started to take a downward turn. He repeatedly had to be hospitalized for multiple health problems. None of the doctors could get a handle on his exact problem. During one of those times, David almost died from a severe case of pancreatitis. His condition was so life threatening that it was necessary for him to be in the Intensive Care Unit. I was now well into my profession as a social worker, working with critically ill people and their families. My professional experiences gave me the insight of the vital importance of having reconciliation with those that you love before missing the window of opportunity.

As I was on the way to see one of my patients, I passed the hospital where David was a patient. A rather uncomfortable feeling came over me as I realized I was no longer just in the role of social worker. I could not stay the objective observer as someone who was paid to handle difficult family matters, and then go home at five o'clock. Now I was in the role of the brother and family member, the one who needed to be the person to proactively deal with the difficult family issue at hand and build a bridge.

I had an hour before my next appointment and the uncomfortable feeling persisted. I knew that to rid myself of it, I had to see my brother. I also knew in my heart that I did love him and I wanted to clear the way for a better relationship. I went to his room and found him lying in bed awake, watching a Lakers basketball game. He did acknowledge I was there and went back to watching television. I asked him if I could have a moment of his time to discuss something that had weighed heavily on my mind. He consented, and I expressed how much I really loved and cared for him. I wanted his forgiveness for whatever I had done that drove us apart. I would be willing to do what I needed to repair any ill feelings between us. As usual, David said very little, and showed little interest, or so I thought. As

I left the hospital, my uncomfortable feeling lifted and I knew with confidence that I had done everything within my power to try and mend our relationship.

David returned home, but still I felt that nothing between us had changed. It was then I realized, for myself, that just doing my part in the forgiveness process can unleash its healing power, if only for my benefit.

About a month passed since our meeting in the hospital, and I received a letter from David. In the letter, he told me how much it meant to him to have me visit him in the hospital, and how he understood exactly what I was asking of him that day. He had always looked up to me as a positive influence in his life and was truly thankful for my part in his life. He concluded that he had always been jealous of me, since I was my parent's biological child, and he wasn't. He went on to say how sorry he was for having those jealous feelings and now wanted my forgiveness. For the next five years, our friendship grew stronger — even stronger than it had been in our childhood.

David finally passed away after multiple medical complications. My only regret was that I didn't approach David earlier so we could have had the relationship we both enjoyed in our later years together. Out of this experience, I learned that our reconciliations need to be made sooner rather than later — as we truly are meant to live with the highest level of love we are capable of having for one another. We will know when this kind of love has encircled us, because its presence is unconditionally felt.

My mother went through David's room after he died and found a letter that his biological mother had written, asking him to please contact her. David never did contact his birth mother because of his resentment toward her for giving him up as a child. But now that he was gone, a rather strong feeling came to my mother that prompted her to make contact with his estranged family members. She informed his mother that their son had passed away and she extended her an invitation to his memorial service. She followed her instincts, knowing that the mother who had given him life needed closure and reconciliation on a past choice she had regretted.

Contact with his family was made and the invitation was received with gratitude and open arms. David's biological mother, three sisters, and one brother showed up to his service — to bid farewell to the son and brother they never had the opportunity to know.

I observed something truly amazing that day at David's memorial, as his two mothers finally came together: one that gave him life and the other that gave him a life. My mother demonstrated her compassionate nature to all in attendance as she suspended her judgment toward another who gave her child away, a mother who would have been expected to have the same nurturing instincts as she did. Instead of feelings of judgment and condemnation, there were feelings of compassion toward another human being who, for whatever reason, had turned against her own natural mothering instincts because of overriding emotional turmoil and pain.

After the day ended, we were able to understand that difficult times had come upon David's birth-mother that resulted in her being unable to physically care for her disabled son. It became clear from getting to know a little bit about her life that she had been living with guilt from her past. It also became quite clear that if she had the opportunity to do an encore performance, she would have made a different choice.

This led to our personal realization that we all make life choices that we would not make if we had the chance to do it over again. Our past regrets are what make us human as we all have some kind of trial-and-error learning curves. In no way should this ever be used as an excuse for our misguided choices, but it surely can be used as a universal justification for the human entitlement of forgiveness and understanding.

We may have difficulty fully comprehending why others could put themselves into such a place as to give up a child they were supposed to love and care for. But what we were able to fully comprehend is the importance of being able to suspend our judgment of other human beings when we don't really know their particular circumstances — especially when it is literally impossible for any of us to feel their pain and suffering.

On reflecting back on my life, what a blessing and high honor it was to have that little boy, with holes in his pants and in a wheelchair, show up in my life. It was this initial encounter that would later teach me in my adult life that people, no matter what their background or circumstances, have the capacity to clear the way to make room for reconciliation. And more importantly, they should be given this almost sacred opportunity, sooner rather than later, because life is both short and precious.

We were also all taught the valuable lesson that no matter what we may have done in our past we are deserving of genuine understanding and forgiveness. As a result of reaching out and understanding, David's birth-mother was able to express that she now could return home with a little more peace and resolve. I know with certainty that if my brother and friend were present in spirit at his memorial, he would have found it within his heart to come to this same compassionate understanding — forgiving those he felt had once abandoned him, just as I saw my mother do as she built the bridge called forgiveness.

Conclusion

Forgiveness is like a magnet that draws people back together. When we forgive and are forgiven, the past, present, and future merge as one timeless moment, and love and peace encircle us with its rays of brightness and hope. At certain times in our lives, these feelings can be so strong and empowering that we come to a higher knowledge that love really is the glue that holds the universe together and that it can only keep its adhesive quality through the process of forgiveness. Any negative preconceived ideas, judgments, and beliefs about one another, as well as ourselves, suddenly shift as we decide to love rather than hate; understand rather than judge; or demonstrate compassion instead of being apathetic. The old outdated structures of guilt and resentment are imploded to clear the way for the new skyline of peace, love, and above all, pure joy. It is these shifts in our perspective that are the miracles that can heal our lives if we only allow!

Circumstances are the rulers of the weak;
they are but instruments of the wise.

—Samuel Lover

Chapter 11

The Healing Power of Perspective

FOR MOST OF us, we would desire to be absolved from our life's challenges and adversities by some miraculous fix-it scheme or cure and live happily ever after. But then again some of us would have liked our American Literature teacher to dismiss us from class with an "A+" on our final report card without learning the profound writings of Emerson. In looking back, we may regret that we didn't take advantage of this time to increase our knowledge of the enlightened words of this famous writer instead of taking the easy way out. We will always find that with our best efforts, nothing is lived in vain no matter what the outcome. And so it is with all of our life experiences, especially the difficult ones. I am positive that if we were to reflect back, we would find that many of our most difficult challenges or adversities, while not cured or suddenly taken away, have facilitated not only our personal growth, but the growth of those around us as well. Every one of us, whether or not we have the big cure readily available, either through the advances in medical science or some other miraculous source, we "ALL" have the ability to be healed.

For a healing to occur in our lives, nothing external to us necessarily has to change, and nothing needs to be outwardly manipulated to change our circumstances. Rather, healing is something that can only happen inwardly as our perspective is enlarged to accommodate a deeper understanding of our experiences as they are put into a broader context on the journey to claiming our full potential. Some of the biggest barriers do surface because we are so preoccupied with finding the big cure that we fail to recognize when we are actually healed. We would scarcely want to be dismissed from the curriculum of hard knocks if we knew that within it was included some of the greatest opportunities for unlocking the healing power of perspective. It is then we can look back on the road we have traveled, and no matter how bumpy that road has been, we will be compelled to admit that we are a better person for having stayed the course.

The Freedom to Choose

ALL OF THE experiences discussed in this book have absolutely nothing to do with the "big cure." Rather, they have to do with a willingness to change the way in which we view our lives.

There's nothing extraordinarily mystical or supernatural to look for. There's nothing outside us we need to possess or take control of in order to replace our lens, through which we view our life experiences. In my observations of living with a physical disability, I finally realized that to ease our adversities, we have to allow the very real and present human spirit to have the opportunity to enlarge our perspective on whatever we may be dealing.

I have to admit there were numerous times that I threw inner-tantrums, demanding the "big cure" to take away all my problems and perceived road blocks, without having to expend any of my own personal effort. I failed to acknowledge that it was up to me to choose to creatively adapt and step beyond those personal problems by becoming my personal best.

Paramount in my self-realization process was the fact that I had to accept being my personal best, disability and all. In retrospect, it took longer for me to be healed because I failed to acknowledge that true healing is not necessarily an absence of adversity — but the ability to perceive the adversity from a heightened vantage point. It is the technology of the human spirit that already resides within us that ensures that irrespective of our individual circumstances, "ALL" of us have the innate ability to be genuinely healed. When we acknowledge this "majestic" truth about this shining light included in our humanness, we bounce back!

Perspective is just like a rubber band, only with unlimited elasticity. No matter what our outward circumstances may be, we have the complete freedom to either choose to expand or contract our perspective. Yes! How we view our circumstances is never held captive to external forces. It is totally left up to us, and to see it any other way is to play the "blame-game," delaying the healing within of which we are all capable. As discussed in Chapter 3, blaming or taking the victim role leads to a downward spiral, ultimately leaving us with a contracted perspective. No healing is possible if our direction is not changed. This does not mean that we should forcefully suppress feelings of blame or victimhood when they surface. But rather, we should accept those feelings as the necessary steps toward healing, with the inner-knowledge that we can ultimately transcend them. The question then becomes, not if we have these feelings, but how can we choose to use them to build and edify ourselves to complete our "Perfect Circles"?

None of us is exempt from adversity. We've all known people who attribute the absence of adversity with living a better life than others, or somehow being more in touch with the spiritual laws of cause and effect. While keeping away from the things we know will eventually tear us down, and keeping affirmative thoughts will most certainly minimize the amount of adversity we are confronted with, it will not absolve us from it. We cannot honestly think the millions of people imprisoned in the World War II concentration camps deserved or created their unfortunate plight. While our actions and thoughts can't necessarily get rid of adversity, they can most certainly elevate us to see beyond the misfortune and tragedy to the greater purpose that is intended to make us stronger.

The world renowned concentration camp survivor, Viktor E. Frankl and author of the book, *Man's Search for Meaning*, made some profound discoveries about the resiliency of the human spirit. He observed in both himself and his fellow prisoners that even though every one of their tangible freedoms had been stripped away, there was one freedom that was not, nor could ever be taken — the freedom to choose how we will inwardly respond or view our set of circumstances. Those who were able to withstand the pain and torture inflicted upon them by their captors, and ultimately survive, were the ones who found a deeper meaning beyond their suffering and that made them stronger and more refined. When all is said and done, the human spirit proves that if used to its fullest capacity, it is not subject to tangible restraints put upon it by even the most heinous of circumstances. When we look back on our lives, some of the most important questions will be answered. How they are answered will ultimately depend on how far we choose to stretch the rubber band called perspective.

An Important Question

MY UNCLE, JACK Rushton, is one of the brightest examples of how healing does and can occur in our lives as the human spirit soars above the turbulence of adversity. Until 1989, Jack had a fully functioning body and was very athletic. He played everything from basketball to baseball. He had a wonderful marriage and raised six successful children. Jack was also very active in his community and already a great teacher of faith and inspiration in his church. He exemplified, in the eyes of those within his sphere of influence, everything a human being is capable of becoming.

On the last day of his summer vacation, at Laguna Beach, California, he was enjoying the day with his family — body surfing with his children. His life and the lives of those who loved him would change dramatically as he hit his head on a rock protruding from the shallow water of the shoreline. Jack remembers very little about the incident, other than the shock that came over his body and the washing machine effect of the waves crashing over him. The paramedics pronounced him dead on the scene, but after considerable effort, they were able to revive him.

He remembers waking up in the hospital, paralyzed, unable to move or talk. The first thing he remembers hearing from one of the nurses is, "I wonder if they did him any favor by bringing him back." This would be the question of all questions that Jack would eventually answer as his evolving perspective would bring about a miraculous healing for both him and his family.

Jack had severed his spinal cord and would have to live the rest of his life on a respirator. That machine would do something for him that we all too often take for granted — breathe! His entire body, from the neck down, was paralyzed. He would be a quadriplegic for the rest of his life. Except for the bodily functions of chewing, swallowing and talking, that were restored only after intensive rehabilitative therapy, he would be dependent on not only a machine to breathe for him, but on everyone around him to do everything that he was once able to do for himself. Jack's life, along with the rest of his family's, changed as a result of that one moment at the beach.

The miracle of healing began for his entire family as they were able to quickly adjust their lives to rise to the occasion to assist their father with all that he needed. The love that already existed in their home before the accident made it possible for them to transform tragedy into new opportunities for personal growth.

For my uncle Jack, his healing did not come without once again treading the rough waters of despair and depression. His mind, being stronger and more coherent than ever, made this reality challenge him even harder as he felt trapped and isolated in a body that could no longer function on its own or do anything that it was once able. His supportive wife, Joann, recalls how Jack emotionally turned inward — with very little communication to or with anyone. Jack remembers asking himself, as well as his loving Higher Power that he had always had faith in and faithfully served, "why me?" But with no real answer, he felt abandoned. As discussed in Chapter 3, Jack had hit the bottom of his personal pit to the point that it started to erode the strong relationship he had with his caring wife.

The only way for Jack to begin his upward ascent was to now utilize his unwavering faith that was now needed more than ever. He began with constant prayer and meditation, surrendering to his Higher Power that he unequivocally knew had the ability to heal him in a way that even the most advanced medical science could not. He felt that while the doctors had done all they could to cure him; there was yet more healing to be done. Today, Jack feels that he was indeed healed by the transcendent powers that are higher than this world. But not in the form of a cure in which all of his bodily functions were suddenly restored to their perfect state. Rather, he feels that a loving and compassionate Higher Power instilled within him an expanded awareness of his situation and how it could be used for the growth of not only himself, but of others around him. Jack explains that while he still sometimes has his down days, as we all do, he no longer feels the heaviness of isolation and abandonment that he once did. Instead of asking the desperate question of "why me?" he can now ask with a gentle demeanor and a sense of the sacred, "why not me?"

Jack refers to the day of his accident as his "other birthday." He makes such a reference because even though he was 50 when it happened, it marked a total change in his life. He explains that he has lived two separate lives, the one prior to the accident and the one after.

He had no choice but to creatively adapt to his new body or "second life" that brought about a whole new set of challenges and circumstances with which he never dreamed he would have to contend. While at times he does mourn the loss of his first life, he sees the new depth and inner expansion that has been created as a result of his disability. New relationships and understandings that could not have been formed, except through a physically disabled body, have added to his worldly experience.

He surprisingly says, in a sincere and enlightened manner, "I wouldn't trade my second life for anything because it has brought me more interpersonal growth that makes it worth living. In looking at it in this way, I don't have to see my 'other birthday' with any regret or bitterness." To contemplate such a statement, we can come to know that no matter what happens to us, we always have the ability to journey to higher ground to see our life's experiences, both the good and the bad, from a different perspective.

No matter how well my uncle lived up to the point of his tragic accident, he still sees himself subject to the same adversities of life as does everyone else. He does not claim exempt status from life's tragedies. He never blamed the Higher Power that he has grown to personally know so well throughout his life, or felt that his spiritual investment didn't pay high enough dividends.

His spiritual lens has allowed him to see his world as purposeful, with tragedy, however intensely undesirable, as something that pays high dividends of continued growth and personal refinement. Because of this unwavering faith, and ability to see beyond tragedy to the opportunities for stretching into realms he never fathomed he could, he has caused those within his sphere of influence to do the same. Others kept the faith because Jack did and there were no excuses for victimhood. Those who have had the opportunity and privilege of knowing and helping Jack say throughout their experience they have learned greater tolerance, understanding, and compassion for those around them as well as themselves.

During one of my many conversations with Jack, I had the privilege of acquiring some of his most important insights. The one big lesson he learned throughout the years of living in a disabled body is the vital role love plays in sustaining life.

He has had the opportunity to visit and comfort people in nursing homes, in a physical condition similar to his, without family and friends to care for them. During the course of these visits, he has observed that many of these people, although sometimes having lesser medical complications, have not had the same longevity and quality of life as has Jack. Jack has attributed his longevity to the fact that he has received the personalized loving care of not only his wife and children, but also those who willingly provided their continued love and support. He knows that without this unconditional love, he would have died within a short time after his accident. In a profound summation of a lesson well learned, he concluded that meeting by saying, "Through my own experience, I have come to know love is the force that keeps us alive."

Upon returning home after six months of intensive rehabilitation and fighting for his life, Jack encountered another outpouring of love and compassion by his friends and neighbors. As his newly purchased wheelchair-accessible van pulled around the street corner — there was a celebration of his life. Large banners were held by at least a hundred people who gathered for the sole purpose to cheer on and welcome their friend, neighbor, and father back home. As Jack rolled up and out the ramp, he saw family and friends from his church and neighborhood waiting for him to see their work of love. They had collectively donated days of their skills and labor to modify his home, making the accommodations necessary for daily living. Accessible space was made so he could continue writing with specialized computer modifications. This would enable him to remain a spiritual teacher — as he has so faithfully devoted his entire life.

Jack has continued using this space as his friends had intended it to be, enriching the minds and spirits of those who look to him as an example of how adversity can be overcome, and first and foremost, how true spirituality does pay the dividends it promises.

Those people gave their time and effort to give something back to another human being who has dedicated so much of his own life in the service of others. And so it is with the nature of both giving and receiving, as we give, we receive and vice versa. This is just one of many examples of how love has sustained his life.

Jack is a true teacher of how love, laughter, and lightheartedness are mutually essential components for healing to occur. He takes life seriously while being able to add a touch of humor. When a potential life-threatening event comes his way, he takes a moment to look back on it and lighten the load through laughter. He recalled with a chuckle in his voice and a smile on his face, one particular incident that could have ended his life. One time, as Jack was lying in his hospital bed being attended to by the nurse, the hose supplying oxygen to his lungs became disconnected.

He calmly alerted the nurse by saying, "air, air." Being that he has a receding hairline, the nurse thoughtfully replied, "Sir, you have plenty of hair." Jack repeated his plea for assistance as the nurse repeated her reassuring comment, as his air hose lay disconnected and his life was slowly seeping away. At this point, he had no air to speak another word, and he was quite sure he was going to die. He vividly recalls that at that point he almost wanted to laugh as he couldn't believe his last minutes on earth were going to be spent in this way. It was then that another nurse walked in the room and realized what had happened. She quickly re-connected the hose and he resumed his normal breathing.

Jack recalls this incident, not to bring to our attention how negligent hospital staff can be, and play the helpless victim, but rather, to lighten up our life by making us laugh. Yes, the nurse was at fault and this situation could have ended his life, and at the time it was happening he did not take it lightly. Now he is able to look back on this long since past experience and see only the comic relief side.

When we hear him tell this story, we are sure to laugh not at him, but with him. To be around someone in Jack's physical condition, one might think they would feel the heaviness of life's random tragedies that can happen to any one of us. But quite the contrary! Being around him makes one feel lighter and brings clarity that our perspective can be untouched by life's tragic circumstances.

Looking beyond our personal world and into the realm of others provides us with the needed healing for our soul. Jack's affirmative influence and perseverance reaches others through the use of e-mails that he sends to people who are experiencing similar life challenges — and to those who are not. His family and friends are privileged to read what he terms "observations" that he has made in his life of living in a quadriplegic body.

After getting a brief glimpse of looking through Jack's eyes, it became quite clear that his personal healing came not from the "big cure," but from a shift in perspective. His stories relate to us as they have within them the commonalities we each share in becoming stronger through adversity. Jack extends the invitation to others to widen their own outlook, as he reaches out with his "observations" of how this is not only possible, but indeed very real.

On the bumpy road of adversity, Jack and those around him have truly had the opportunity to learn the importance of acceptance, tolerance, and most importantly love — in holding all of life together. The life of my uncle leaves us with the profound message that while none of us is exempt from adversity, if we can learn and grow from it, our life will not have been lived in vain. While the big cure may not be anywhere in sight, the healing power of perspective most certainly is.

Jack has answered that one important question, posed by his nurse on the day of his second birth, by saying, "It's good to be alive!"

Conclusion

NOW THAT THE school bell has rung and the day is over, it is time to reflect back to see if we have learned something of enduring worth. The big question should not be whether or not we got through the day unscathed or without discomfort. Instead, did we use all of our moments of opportunity and inner-resources to widen our perspective, even in the times we desperately wanted to exit the classroom? And although unwanted, did we reverse the tides of negativity forced upon us through adversity, sometimes tragedy, and change into a positive current that takes us safely ashore?

Our unique individual life scripts create the great masterpieces that make all the class time spent well worth the trouble and effort. When we can say that healing is within our grasp, not because anything external has necessarily changed, but because we have widened our perspective, then we have creatively adapted to whatever circumstance is put before us. Then, when the first bell of the day rings to summon our undivided attention to the curriculum especially designed for us, we will be honored to not only show up — but to give it our all. In life, you get out what you put into it! **Remember, in "Perfect Circles," what goes around, comes around!**

God grant me the serenity to accept the things I cannot change; courage to change the things I can; and wisdom to know the difference.

THE SERENITY PRAYER
—REINHOLD NIEBUHR

Chapter 12

The Perfectly Imperfect Ending

WHILE I WOULD like to write the perfect conclusion to this book, one that gives answers and solutions to all life's problems and adversities, the hard-hitting reality is — I can't! I can't offer any magic formulas or ancient passwords that have been handed down from more advanced civilizations to end the human plight of adversity and suffering. If I could, then *Perfect Circles* would have the perfect ending and I would be the ultimate self-help guru. And you would never need to buy another self-help book again!

Being that this book has no such ending, then why does it have such a title? Shouldn't it more appropriately be called *Imperfect Circles*, or better yet, *Just Another Self-Help-Book that Can't Fix My Life*?

My only claim to fame is my participation in a world that offers textures of experiences for potential growth and development. I can not say at the conclusion of this book that I have never fallen prey to feelings of hopelessness. I have had what I thought were very turbulent periods and I expect there will be more. Yes, like all of us, I have ridden life's roller coaster and had those white knuckle moments — some lasting longer than others. But as with all of our personal stories, our claim to the heroic roles we play is not because we flew faster than a speeding bullet or leaped tall buildings in a single bound. True heroism is achieved when we see in each experience, the good along with the bad and big along with small opportunities to grow. In doing so, we create enduring foundations and stretch our perspectives further than we thought possible. We don't stop the inevitable forces or changes from happening, but we view them from higher ground. Now **that's** true healing!

The "Perfect" Paradox

SINCE I SINCERELY want to leave you, the reader, with something more than a series of heartfelt stories about overcoming life's challenges, I will offer a final summation of what "Perfect Circles" are and are not.

Let me start by saying what they are not, so that you have a comparison to see its paradoxical nature. "Perfect Circles" do not represent our wholeness if they are dependent on sitting atop a mountain in a 24/7 meditative state and being at one with the universe. The perfect day is not one in which our peanut butter and jelly sandwiches look nice and neat, and all United States postal workers put on friendly smiles as they attend to our immediate needs. While those circumstances might be nice, they are not what makes up reality. The perfect day is not defined as one free from adversity and challenges, but rather, one in which we have acquired more inner strength and put a little more brick and mortar on our foundation that is always a work in progress! The processes of life and how we move through it is more instrumental in our long-term emotional well-being than getting to some arbitrary destination.

If "Perfect Circles" does not stand for being in a "perfect" state of oneness with the entire universe, bringing us to permanent bliss, then what else could it possibly represent? Simply put, the "Perfect Circle" is a symbol of our acceptance of our innate wholeness and worth as unique "human beings." We can then move forward and become stronger — not despite our challenges and adversities, but because of them! Since most of us don't have 24/7 access to a compass to draw geometrically precise circles, we might as well accept drawing the imperfect ones and move forward for having the opportunity to do so.

Allowing "Perfect" to be Redefined

THE TERM "PERFECT" as used in this book is not a specific criteria or ideal that one can be compared to, but rather, a measurement that determines one's individualized level of perfection. The potential each one of us can reach need not be compared to anyone else's because abilities and disabilities vary from one person to the next. Every person has his own set of assets and challenges that makes his contributions unique. True potential and our individualized "perfect" state is reached when we are willing to creatively adapt to whatever is put before us — becoming our "personal best" instead of someone else's perception of our personal best.

We ultimately come to the realization that the things we want erased from our lives, our weaknesses and adversities, are the very things that make us stronger. It is only then that the familiar saying, "Where there's a will, there's a way," becomes more than just a motto, but a living reality.

Our perspective of both ourselves and each other expands, seeing all of our perceived human imperfections, be they physical or emotional, as opportunities for our personal growth, instead of something to be dreaded and a rationale for not being able to truly live life to its fullest. These opportunities don't have to be welcomed or liked, but merely recognized when they appear — keeping the upward and forward momentum with the power of perspective and affirmative expectation.

The curveballs we are sure to be thrown, once we think we have conquered the world, are more opportunities to test the strength of the human spirit. Life changes and transitions, such as aging and tragic occurrences that lessen our abilities, are transformed into opportunities to widen our perspectives, and allow us to reach beyond ourselves to explore our untapped human potential.

Individual conflicts and even conflicts between countries are transformed into opportunities for coming to mutual understanding — tearing down barriers and realizing the healing power of forgiveness. All we need to do is look beyond the layers of preconceived ideas and beliefs formed from years of both individual and collective conditioning. As our perspective changes, so does our world!

Our unfortunate life circumstances are viewed through the lens of hope rather than hopelessness and we start to see the good that already exists all around. We start to recognize the people in our lives who really do perform random acts of kindness and make our world a better place to be. No matter what our disabilities or perceived barriers may be, none of us is exempt from being an active participant in this dynamic process. Once we comprehend the term "perfect" in this way, we have no excuse but to weave ourselves into our personal best.

True healing comes when we view life from an expanded perspective — not by measuring our worth and accomplishments with some preconceived ideal that we, ourselves, can not possibly reach. Our peanut butter and jelly dough ball can become the perfect sandwich — if we view it that way. After all, has anyone ever come up with official specifications on how to create a peanut butter and jelly sandwich?

Completing the "Circle"

THE "CIRCLE" REPRESENTS accepting our flaws and imperfections so we can move beyond our frustrations. We feel as if we are no longer a lone traveler on foreign soil — because our imperfect humanness is part of our personal best; or, better yet, our perfect selves.

As we figuratively draw our circles without the aid of a compass precisely guiding our hand, we don't condemn ourselves if our hand jumps or goes slightly off course, making our lines into an unintended shape or design. When our circle is complete, we take the opportunity to reflect, looking beyond its perceived imperfections.

At first, we may be very tempted to retrace our lines, making them look more like the perfect circles we had envisioned in our preconditioned mind, or we may decide to throw the drawing away. But if we really are to accept our humanity, we will begin to come to that "Majestic Moment" in time where we realize that our circles, like every person's, are never exactly the same.

We have come to know that all of our flaws, challenges, and adversities are the very components that push us in a forward direction and make us stronger. We build upon our experiences, instead of trying to shun or remove them. In place of regret, we see opportunities to learn. When feelings of hopelessness and self-loathing set in because of undesirable or uncomfortable transitions, we take these events as the stage for the resiliency of the human spirit to play its part.

As Shakespeare so eloquently said, "All the world's a stage, And all the men and women merely players." At the conclusion of our final act, the magnitude of our standing ovation or inner peace and contentment will solely depend on how we accepted our "Perfect Circles" as well as others.

Did we play our part without regret, feeling like we did not measure up or did we learn from every experience? Did we see the beautiful tapestries because of how we creatively adapted in a positive way to overcome our adversities and differences and make them stepping stones — instead of a stumbling block?

The Big Finish

IN ORDER TO evolve into all we're meant to be, we need to first accept where we are at this very moment. Moving forward means being perfectly comfortable with and accepting and molding ourselves from our personal best. What a **perfect** paradox!

Accepting our perfect and imperfect selves leaves us absolutely no room for rationalizations to engage in self-loathing and victimhood. If we can reflect back on all of our life's experiences — with the awareness that not one experience was lived in vain, then we have come in with **the** first-place trophy!

Our car is allowed to roll off the assembly line and enter the race. To win the race, we don't have to have the flashiest or fastest car, or one with the biggest, roundest tires; only the ability to answer life's call to create our "Perfect Circles."

What could be a more **perfect** ending?

About the Author

JOHN MICHAEL STUART is a motivational speaker for schools, corporate events, church groups, and service organizations across the country. He has served as a spokesperson for the March of Dimes and Easter Seals. John received his master's degree in social work from the University of Nevada, Las Vegas, in 1997 and has since worked as a case manager and counselor in the hospice, hospital, and rehabilitation health venues.

John was born with cerebral palsy, a neurological condition that has affected his motor coordination. He resides in Las Vegas and enjoys frequent weekend retreats at the family home in Lake Arrowhead, California.